PRAYING
SUNDAY PS

Richard Atherton

a redemptorist publication

(Year A)

Published by Redemptorist Publications
Alphonsus House Chawton Hants GU34 3HQ

First printed November 2001
Reprinted November 2003

Design: Orchid Design

ISBN 0 85231 255 5

Printed in Britain

Redemptorist
PUBLICATIONS

Contents

Foreword

On the day of his resurrection, Jesus appeared to his friends and spoke to them about everything that had been written of him 'in the law of Moses, in the prophets and in the psalms'[1] and then 'he opened their minds to understand the scriptures' (Luke 24:44-45). The psalms therefore throw light on Jesus and his mission. Perhaps it would be more accurate to say that as a result of his coming the psalms have taken on a richer meaning; their full potential has been realised. In the audacious words of a modern writer, before the birth of Christ, the psalms 'were like unconsecrated hosts, destined for a fulfilment beyond themselves'.[2]

It is hardly surprising then that in the liturgical renewal which has taken place since the Second Vatican Council, a psalm, or at least part of a psalm, has become a regular feature of the Mass. Indeed, the *General Instruction on the Roman Missal* describes the responsorial psalm as 'an integral part of the Liturgy of the Word'. It is one way in which the whole congregation becomes actively involved in this part of the Mass, a way in which they express their acceptance of the Word of God. At the same time it enables them to reflect on the other readings and even come to a clearer understanding of them. Ideally it should be sung, but, even when spoken, its poetic language often lingers on in the memory and so enables us to carry the psalm over into daily life.

The three-yearly cycle of Sunday readings is based on the gospel, which is taken either from Matthew (Year A), Mark (Year B) or Luke (Year C).[3] Strictly speaking, the responsorial psalm is chosen because of its connection with the first reading, usually a passage from the Old Testament, but since that first reading itself is chosen to fit in with the gospel – by offering, for example, an Old Testament foreshadowing of it or an Old Testament contrast with it – the responsorial psalm can be said to reflect the overall theme of the Mass. (The second reading runs an independent course in that it normally consists, Sunday by Sunday, of one section after another of a New Testament letter, yet even so it is often possible to discover some link with the other readings of the day.)

This book has been written in the conviction that many worshippers find that they are unable to make much of the responsorial psalm 'unless [like the Ethiopian servant in Acts 8:31] someone guides me'. The guidance offered in this book for each Sunday falls into three sections. The first is a brief summary of the three readings and an introductory note to the psalm, indicating the common theme that re-echoes through the Liturgy of the Word on that particular day and so providing the context in which the psalm is to be understood. The second section attempts to explain the original meaning of the psalm and its application to the theme of the day. It is entitled 'Prayerful Ponderings'; in the gospel Mary is revealed as a woman who pondered things, treasured them, in her heart (Luke 2:19, 51). She brought that pondering, prayerful approach to her own use of the Psalter. Such an approach is surely the key to discovering the true value of the responsorial psalm. The third and final section is simply a brief prayer which attempts to summarise what has gone before in prayerful form.

It is hoped that the book will be of particular help to Church Readers. If they are to fulfil their task worthily, they need to read not only with competence but also with conviction, and conviction presupposes a familiarity, a prayerful familiarity, with what they read. Preachers also have been in mind in the writing of these pages. It is a sad fact that though many books have been written to help preachers with their Sunday homily, few offer anything more than a passing reference to the responsorial psalm. However, this book is also aimed at helping the general body of worshippers to derive greater benefit from this part of the Mass. They might, for example, prepare for their Sunday Mass by reading through the appropriate passage in advance, perhaps also reading through the whole psalm in their Bible, since what is given in the liturgy is usually only an excerpt from a much longer song. Similarly, they might refer to the book in the course of the following week in order to prolong their reflection on the Sunday readings. As its title suggests, this book will have achieved its purpose if it leads readers not only to the understanding but also, and above all, to the praying of the Sunday psalm.

Notes

1) The Law, the prophets and the psalms (where 'the psalms' includes all the Writings) are the three divisions of the Hebrew Scriptures

2) Maria Boulding, *The Coming of God* (SPCK, 1994), p.98.

3) St John's Gospel features on the Sundays of Lent and Eastertide in each of the three years. Because the Gospel of Mark is shorter than the others, St John also provides the gospel reading for the seventeenth to the twenty-first Sunday of Year B.

Acknowledgements

I offer my thanks to Rosemary Gallagher of Redemptorist Publications for her encouragement in the work, and to my brother Bernard for enriching this book with his attractive art-work.

ADVENT

*A shoot
shall spring
from the
stock of
Jesse*

ADVENT

'The season of Advent has a twofold character.
It is a time of preparation for Christmas
when the first coming of God's Son... is recalled.
It is also a season when minds are directed by this
memorial to Christ's second coming at the end of time.
It is thus a season of joyful and spiritual expectation'
(General Norms for the Liturgical Year §39)

First Sunday of Advent

The lovely season of Advent, which begins today, is a time to prepare to celebrate the coming of Jesus to humankind, and also to direct our thoughts to the end of time when he will come again in glory to lead us to our true home.

During the first weeks of Advent the emphasis of the liturgy is particularly, though not exclusively, upon the Second Coming. So today's first reading (Isaiah 2:1-5) looks forward to a time when all the world will be gathered together in the peace of God's kingdom, the second (Romans 13:11-14) instructs us to make ready now because the Lord's day is growing ever nearer, and the gospel (Matthew 24:37-44) bids us stay awake so that we may be ready 'when the Son of Man comes'.

Psalm 121,★ the responsorial psalm for today, is particularly apt; it is one of the fifteen 'Psalms of Ascent', so-called because they were sung by the Israelites as they made their pilgrimage way up to Jerusalem for the great feasts – 'up' because Jerusalem stands some 2400 feet above sea-level. (Modern Christian pilgrims to the Holy Land joyfully recite this psalm as the city of Jerusalem comes into view: the moment of arrival is at hand!)

★*There are two ways of numbering the psalms; the one adopted in this book is the one most commonly used in Sunday Missals. The other enumeration is usually one ahead (e.g. Psalm 121 would appear as 122).*

Prayerful Ponderings

'I rejoiced when I heard them say: "Let us go to God's house".'
Commenting on this verse, St Augustine wrote that just as everything is so 'weighted' that it tends in a particular direction – fire upwards, a stone downwards – and cannot rest till it reaches its 'proper place', so we are (should be) weighted towards God by our love. That is why we remain restless, why we cannot fully rejoice, until we reach the end of our pilgrim journey, until we arrive in 'God's house'.

'And now our feet are standing within your gates, O Jerusalem.'
In the New Testament the city of Jerusalem is used as a symbol for 'the heavenly Jerusalem' which marks the end of our Christian pilgrimage (Hebrews 12:22; Revelation 21:2), where the Lamb is enthroned and where a numberless host is gathered in worship (Revelation 14:1). During Advent we are encouraged to prepare for that day when, with the coming of Christ, we shall find ourselves standing within the gates of that Jerusalem!

'It is there that the tribes go up, the tribes of the Lord. For Israel's law it is, there to praise the Lord's name.'
At the three major annual festivals, Passover, Pentecost and Tabernacles, members of the twelve tribes of Israel would 'go up' to Jerusalem 'there to praise the Lord's name'. The practice was authorised, indeed demnded, by covenant Law (e.g. Exodus 23:14–17).

In this Advent season, the Church, symbolically built upon the twelve tribes in the persons of the twelve apostles, summons us to 'go up' in a spirit of prayer and praise to celebrate the great festival of Christmas.

'There were set the thrones of judgement of the house of David.' The seats of justice had been established in Jerusalem under the Davidic kings, and, according to the prophets, the city had a special responsibility for the maintenance of justice in Israel. And so the pilgrimage season was the ideal period for the settling of disputes among the peoples. Part of our task during this Advent season may well be to try and resolve differences that exist among the people of God in our parish, our neighbourhood – even our own household.

'For the peace of Jerusalem pray: "Peace be to your homes! May peace reign in your walls, in your palaces, peace!" For love of my brethren and friends I say: "Peace upon you!"'
With a play on the name of the city and the Hebrew word for peace (*shalom*), the psalmist begs the people to pray for Jerusalem's peace: first, peace within the family 'homes'; then peace within the city's 'walls' and 'palaces'; and finally peace upon all our 'brethren and friends'. Peace is the first theme mentioned on this first Sunday of Advent (see first reading). What better Christmas gift could we receive, or offer to our brothers and sisters and all our friends, than the blessing of peace? In the measure that we allow Christ to be born in us we shall be able to spread his kingdom of peace to others.

'For love of the house of the Lord I will ask for your good.'
What Jerusalem was for Israelites the Church is for Christians. And so we pray that despite the shortcomings and the scandals, which Jesus warned would come, the Church may be granted *shalom*, that fullness of well-being that will enable it to stand forth as the Sacrament of his Presence in the world.

LET US PRAY: *By your resurrection, Lord, the Church became a new Jerusalem, united by the Spirit. Grant us peace and draw all peoples towards your Church so that together we may share your gifts and render you thanks until that day when we reach the heavenly Jerusalem.*

Second Sunday of Advent

Today Isaiah (11:1-10) speaks of a king, filled with God's spirit, and of the peace and justice he will bring, especially for the poor.

The splendid responsorial psalm, Psalm 71, picks up the same theme; it looks forward to a new era that God will inaugurate through the agency of a king. Though probably composed for the coronation of one of Israel's Davidic kings (David was the first of the royal line) and meant to remind him of his high calling, it opens up such an incredible vista (of a reign, for example, which is everlasting and a peace which is perfect) that it clearly looks towards an ideal king yet to come. In fact Jewish and Christian traditions alike have seen it as portraying the Messianic king foretold by Isaiah.

It is to the coming of that King, Jesus Christ, and of his kingdom that John the Baptist directs our thoughts in today's gospel (Matthew 3:1-12). However, that King is to come again at the end of human history. In the meantime, as Paul reminds us in the second reading (Romans 15:4-9), our hope is to be sustained by what 'was written long ago in the scriptures'.

Prayerful Ponderings

'**O God, give your judgement to the king, to a king's son your justice, that he may judge your people in justice and your poor in right judgement.**'

In ancient times the king was much more than a figurehead: his rule had practical implications in the daily life of every member of society, and so Israel prays that its new king will be a person of integrity, one whose dealings are based on 'justice' so that he treats everyone, and especially the 'poor' and lowly, with fairness. Israel prayed for such a king, we have such a King – and more besides, for not only is he a King of justice and integrity but a King whose rule is one of love: the Child of Bethlehem will prove himself 'King of love on Calvary'.

'**In his days justice shall flourish and peace till the moon fails.**'
Other kingdoms and empires come and go, even those that look as though they will last for ever. Only his is an everlasting kingdom; it will endure, in the delightful words of the psalmist, 'till the moon fails'. It is a kingdom which exists for the promotion of goodness and human well-being: 'I have come that they may have life, and have it abundantly' (John 10:10).

'**He shall rule from sea to sea, from the Great River to earth's bounds.**'
'Go therefore and make disciples of all nations' (Matthew 28:18-20).

Our King's reign is not only until the end of time, but also to the ends of the world, or – since the psalmist thought of the world as an island surrounded by water – 'from sea to sea'; or, more probably, taking the Euphrates, the largest river known to the psalmist, as a central point – from there to the ends of the earth.

'For he shall save the poor when they cry and the needy who are helpless. He will have pity on the weak and save the lives of the poor.'
The special concern of this King of kings is for the poor and needy (and not only the financially poor). It is not surprising that our sisters and brothers in the developing world are attracted to the psalms, which so often mirror their own plight and prayer. 'He shall save the poor when they cry' – but not if we in the wealthy West sit idly by and wait for things to happen. At the same time we need to recognise our own poverty, for unless we do we shall place ourselves beyond his saving help.

'May his name be blessed for ever and endure like the sun.'
Such a king as described in this psalm will be 'for ever' remembered with reverence and gratitude. Jesus taught us to pray each day, 'thy kingdom come'. It is a way of expressing our desire that 'his name' (he and all he stands for) be 'blessed', that is, recognised, praised and thanked. But, like St Thomas More, we need to add: 'The things I pray for, good Lord, give me grace to labour for.'

'Every tribe shall be blessed in him, all nations bless his name.'
We dare not forget that if all peoples are to experience the blessing of God's concern for them, justice for the poor must always be on

our agenda. Our eternal future depends upon it, for when the King comes again, this time as Judge, he will want to know how we have treated 'the least of these who are members of my family'.

LET US PRAY: *Lord, may your Son's kingdom come so that the world may know peace, the poor may receive justice, and all people bless your holy name.*

Third Sunday of Advent

Today's first reading (Isaiah 35:1-6,10) was originally addressed to the people of Israel during the long days of exile; it promises that though, in their misery and suffering, they are like a dry barren desert, when God comes to save them the desert will be transformed into a flourishing garden.

The note of rejoicing at the end of the first reading is taken up by Psalm 145, today's responsorial psalm, which is a joyous song of praise. 'Alleluia' is its opening plea and the psalmist pledges to sing praise to God all life long. However, he is not unaware of human suffering around. Indeed the psalmist praises God especially because – this is where the responsorial psalm begins – he, unlike the powerful ones of this world, is faithful, has a special concern for the marginalised; only he can offer an answer to the world's hopes by bringing it justice and peace.

If in the first reading all creation seems to be bursting with joy because of God's coming, a coming associated with miracles on behalf of the sick and the suffering, in the gospel (Matthew 11:2-11) Jesus points to the healing miracles of his own ministry in order to assure John that he is indeed the Messiah whom John has heralded and for whose sake the herald will soon lay down his life.

In the second reading St James (5:7-10) reminds us that while we await 'the Lord's coming' and the transformation that he will bring, we must be patient, like the farmer who, though he sees nothing, confidently believes that the seed is growing and one day the fruit will appear.

Prayerful Ponderings

'It is the Lord who keeps faith for ever, who is just to those who are oppressed. It is he who gives bread to the hungry, the Lord, who sets prisoners free.'

Some psalms draw a comparison between God and the idols, he the all-powerful, all-compassionate One, they the powerless and compassionless ones. In this psalm the comparison is between God and the so-called powerful people (like those who, though small in numbers, corner most of the world's wealth), referred to earlier in the psalm as 'the princes' of the people; they are unreliable helpers. The trust of the poor must be lodged in God for it is only he 'who keeps faith for ever'.

'It is the Lord who gives sight to the blind, who raises up those who are bowed down...'

Like the psalmist we boldly proclaim that it is God who is the liberator of the poor and the marginalised. But then we must be ready to share his outlook and concerns. That is why the Synod of Bishops in 1971 made the dramatic statement that the Church's demand for justice for the poor is part of her redemptive mission: 'Action on behalf of justice and participation in the transformation of the world fully appear to us as a constitutive dimension of the preaching of the gospel.'

'...the Lord, who protects the stranger and upholds the widow and orphan.'

In Israel 'the stranger... the widow and orphan' were regarded as typical examples of the socially marginalised and poor. Jesus declared that it was to the poor, in every sense of that word, and to all who are imprisoned, in whatever way, that he had been sent: 'He has sent me to bring good news to the poor, to proclaim liberty to captives' (Luke 4:18).

'It is the Lord who loves the just but thwarts the path of the wicked.'

This line presents the other side of all that has been said so far: if the Lord's concern for the poor is unqualified, 'the wicked' (those who do not have good news for the poor and so have cut off their relationship with God) are in a hazardous position – they are effectively cutting themselves off from his love.

'The Lord will reign for ever, Zion's God, from age to age.'

'Zion', God's dwelling place, came to stand for the city of Jerusalem and eventually to symbolise the Church (ultimately, heaven itself). This final verse guarantees all that has gone before, for it tells us, the new Zion, that our God's reign is for ever and ultimately his will cannot but prevail.

'Come, Lord, and save us.'

What appears in today's first reading as a statement – God 'is coming to save you' – is now turned into a plea and becomes the response to the psalm. But it also serves as an admirable petition for all the days of Advent.

LET US PRAY: *Come, Lord Jesus, come; lover of the poor and the needy, the blind, the lame, and all who are bowed down; teach us to display your generosity in all our dealings with those in need.*

Fourth Sunday of Advent

The final Sunday of Advent. Excitement is growing – the Saviour will soon be here – and today's readings fuel that excitement for they include Isaiah's prophecy (7:10-14) to King Ahaz in the eighth century BC, which tells of a maid who is with child, a child whose name means 'God-is-with-us'; Matthew's account (1:18-24) of the virgin birth of Jesus; and Paul's words (Romans 1:1-7) which sum up perfectly the wonder of Christmas, power clothed in powerlessness: 'the Son of God, who, according to the human nature he took, was a descendant of David'.

The responsorial psalm, Psalm 23, highlights the marvel of this Child's birth by reminding us of his incomparable dignity and, by implication, our unworthiness. Originally, the psalm was an 'entrance liturgy', sung, almost as an examination of conscience, by those about to cross the Temple's threshold.

Prayerful Ponderings

'The Lord's is the earth and its fullness, the world and all its peoples.'
This is more than a statement, it is a profession of faith. Recited by many Jews on the first day of each week, it proclaims that the key truth about all reality is that it is 'the Lord's'; it is his possession because he made it. The 'fullness' of the world – its wonders, great and small – and 'all its peoples' – every man, woman and child that ever has been or ever will be – all, without exception, are his handiwork.

'It is he who set it on the seas; on the waters he made it firm.'
The psalmist's 'simplistic' view is that the Lord securely anchored the earth, visualised as a gigantic disc, upon the always-threatening waters of the deep. We may have more sophisticated and scientific notions, but the essential truth remains: our world finds the ground of its being in the creative will of God.

'Who shall climb the mountain of the Lord? Who shall stand in his holy place?'
Having reflected on God's overwhelming greatness, the pilgrims now ask themselves: who, then, is worthy to enter the Temple of this great God? We too, as we prepare to greet the Lord in the person of a tiny baby, would do well to pose a similar question: how could we ever be ready to receive the Saviour who will soon be in our midst?

'The man with clean hands and pure heart, who desires not worthless things.'

To the question posed by Israel's pilgrims, the response, probably given by a temple priest, is that those who approach the Temple must have 'clean hands' and 'pure heart' or, as we might say, freedom from (at least, desire to be free from) evil in thought and deed. For Christians too an important part of Advent's exercises should be to try and ensure that we have 'clean hands' and 'pure heart' for the One who comes, while always confident that he readily comes to men and women of good will, despite their weaknesses.

'He shall receive blessings from the Lord and reward from the God who saves him.'

All who seek the Lord 'in spirit and truth' are assured of his 'blessings'. For the people of Israel a blessing was almost tangible, the passing of power from God to creature, not unlike the power that went out from Jesus to cure the sick and suffering. The most wonderful 'blessing' and 'reward' that we can receive is the grace by which the 'God who saves us' transforms us into his own divine likeness. In the daring phrase of some of the early Christian Fathers: 'God became man, so that we might become gods.'

'Such are the men who seek him, seek the face of the God of Jacob.'

The pilgrims happily proclaim that they are ready for entry into God's Temple. As we come to the end of our Advent pilgrimage, may we also be able to say that we truly seek our God, earnestly long to gaze upon the Child of Bethlehem, 'the human face of God'.

LET US PRAY: *Lord God, mighty maker of the universe, may our thoughts and deeds bear witness to the eagerness of our longing for you to come and be our Saviour.*

CHRISTMASTIDE

*The
Word
became flesh
Alleluia
Alleluia*

CHRISTMASTIDE

*'The Church considers the
Christmas season, which celebrates
the birth of our Lord and his early
manifestations, second only to the
annual celebration of the
Easter mystery'*
**(General Norms for the
Liturgical Year §32)**

Christmas Midnight

Our Christmas celebrations begin with a prophecy from Isaiah (9:1-7). It tells how the dark distress of those who have suffered invasion will be transformed into light and exhilarating joy, for 'a child has been born for us', a child whose reign will bring justice, peace and every kind of blessing.

The gospel is Luke's account of Jesus' birth (2:1-14). As the fulfilment of Isaiah's prophecy, it spells 'good news of great joy' to all who receive it. However, the letter to Titus (the second reading) will not allow us to forget that if 'God's grace has [now] been revealed' and 'salvation [made] possible for the whole human race', nonetheless the Lord's kingdom has still to come in its fullness and until it does our task is to live lives worthy of the King (Titus 2:11-14).

In the light of the good news brought us this night, it is not surprising that the responsorial psalm is taken from Psalm 95, a joyful invitation to praise. It is one of a category known as 'Enthronement Psalms', which seem to have been specifically composed to acknowledge the kingship of God and may even have accompanied an annual celebration in which God was once again declared to be king. In any event it is a song which truly befits the birth of our King and Lord.

Prayerful Ponderings

'Today a saviour has been born to us; he is Christ the Lord.'
This refrain comes from tonight's gospel; it is the message of the angels over Bethlehem and it sums up our celebration. How can we do other than praise since at last the long-awaited saviour is in our midst? He is (the) Christ, that is, the anointed one, the Messiah. One day, through his death and resurrection, he will reveal that he is also 'Lord', the unique Son of God.

'O sing a new song to the Lord, sing to the Lord all the earth. O sing to the Lord, bless his name.'
Three times over the psalmist exhorts the people, and even 'all the earth', to raise their voice in praise. They are to sing 'a new song', not merely one that is fresh from the press, so to say – though it may indeed be a fresh composition of the psalmist – but rather one that rejoices in God's most recent and most spectacular intervention, an intervention which is to make all things new.

'Proclaim his help day by day, tell among the nations his glory and his wonders among all the peoples.'
We are not only to bless God but also to 'proclaim' him to others and, like the angels of Bethlehem, make known to all his glory and the wonders he has worked. The Hebrew word that lies behind 'proclaim' has a meaning close to 'evangelise', 'proclaim the good

news'. The gospel, and in particular the gospel of Christmas, is God's good news; it is good news not to be kept to ourselves but to be shared with others.

'Let the heavens rejoice and earth be glad, let the sea and all within it thunder praise, let the land and all it bears rejoice, all the trees of the wood shout for joy...'
It is not merely all creatures but all creation that is called upon to join in the praise and the rejoicing: 'the heavens' above and the 'earth' below are to exult; the thundering of 'the sea' is to serve as a paean of praise; everything that grows on dry land, including 'the trees of the wood', is to join in the celebration.

'...at the presence of the Lord, for he comes, he comes to rule the earth.'
And now the reason for all the rejoicing, and the climax of the psalm – the Lord himself at last has come. In the Child in the manger we recognise the Ruler of the universe, and far from it being a threat to human happiness, his presence brings joy and delight to the whole of creation.

'With justice he will rule the world, he will judge the peoples with his truth.'
But this Child whom we shall soon be worshipping is also the Judge who will one day come again to 'rule the world' and to 'judge the peoples' with absolute 'justice'. Amidst our Christmas rejoicing we must not, dare not, forget that all that has happened so far in the history of salvation is in the nature of a preparation for the final judgement of the world and all its peoples, ourselves included.

LET US PRAY: *Lord, through the birth of your Son, our darkness has been turned into light. Help us receive him with love and live lives that will make him known to others.*

The Masses for Christmas Dawn and Christmas Day are to be found in the volumes for Year B and Year C, respectively.

The Holy Family of Jesus, Mary and Joseph

The feast of Christmas is celebrated not for one day but for eight – an octave of days. And on this, the Sunday within that octave, our thoughts and prayers turn first to the Holy Family and then to our own families.

The gospels of the three years – a different one is allotted for each of the A, B and C cycles – give us glimpses of the family life of Jesus, Mary and Joseph. The gospel today (Matthew 2:13-15,19-23) tells of the agonising flight of Jesus and his parents to escape the attentions of King Herod and their eventual return to Nazareth where Jesus would spend his childhood. The other two readings deal, respectively, with the meaning of the fourth commandment, especially where the treatment of elderly parents is concerned (Ecclesiasticus 3:2-6,12-14), and with the cluster of virtues required for happiness within the home (Colossians 3:12-21).

The responsorial psalm, Psalm 127, is particularly apt because it focuses on happy family life. We hear so much these days about the problems and difficulties which beset marriage that it's refreshing to hear a voice raised in joyful praise of its blessings. Of course, Israel's attitudes to the family were conditioned, just as ours are, by the prevailing culture; and there are aspects of the patriarchal society of biblical times which would not be acceptable today: the position of the wife, for example – she was her husband's possession and would address him as 'lord' – would surely fall foul of the sex discrimination laws!

Nonetheless, what shines out is a recognition of the importance of the family as the basic unit of society as well as deep concern for its welfare; who could deny that that recognition and concern are at least as much needed today as ever they were in days gone by? Even the one-sidedness of the psalm – its tendency to see everything through the eyes of the husband/father – is not without value. The psalm was sung as pilgrims made their way to Zion (Jerusalem), which may suggest that whole families went together to worship God. Does not that at least imply that the father has a vital role to play in the religious well-being of the family, and that it shouldn't simply be left to mother to bring up the children in their faith?

That Christ himself became a member of a family, and raised marriage to the dignity of a sacrament, serves only to enhance all that this psalm teaches.

Prayerful Ponderings

'O blessed are those who fear the Lord and walk in his ways!'
A statement of the basic premise which underlies the whole psalm.
It is those who walk in the ways of the Lord and strive to live by
his standards who will receive God's blessing. Christian marriage
involves not two partners but three; it is in close association with
God that a couple are called to live their life together.

**'By the labour of your hands you shall eat. You will be happy
and prosper.'**
It is through their daily labours that husband and wife help to
ensure that their home will prosper and be happy. To have God as
your partner does not relieve you of the obligation of work,
whether that is within the home or outside – or both. But of
course the most vital 'work' of any couple is that of keeping their
love alive and ever deepening.

'Your wife like a fruitful vine in the heart of your house...'
Here is the Israelite ideal: 'a wife like a fruitful vine' – in the Bible
the vine is frequently used as a symbol both of fruitfulness and of
charm – who busies herself 'in the heart of your house', which was
considered the appropriate place for a woman in those days!

'...your children like shoots of the olive, around your table.'
The Israelite ideal included children who would gather around the meal table like so many olive shoots nursed by the parent stem. The anguish that couples experience when they are unable to have children testifies to the fact that children are 'the supreme gift of marriage' (Vatican II). Today we might spare a prayer for those childless couples who long for children.

'Indeed thus shall be blessed the man who fears the Lord.'
Again a reminder that what has been described is ultimately due to God's blessing, and that blessing, the psalmist believes, is reserved for those who reverence the Lord. The form of this verse, as of those that have preceded it, indicates that this is a psalm of instruction in the tradition of the Wisdom books of the Bible.

'May the Lord bless you from Zion all the days of your life!'
A family must not become introspective, concerned only with itself. And so the final verse insists that the domestic family belongs to a larger family, the people of God, who gather in Zion. The Vatican Council described the family as 'the domestic church', the Church in miniature, whose well-being is ordered to the wider community and in particular to the great family of God's people.

LET US PRAY: *Lord God, whose Son became man and grew up in a human family, we thank you for your splendid gifts of love, of marriage and of family life. We ask you to bless families everywhere, to give courage to couples who face difficulties and to draw all Christians to grow in their appreciation of the sacred value of home and family.*

Mary, Mother of God

In becoming man, Jesus took upon himself our humanity in its entirety. That meant that he was born in a particular time and place, that he became a member of a particular race, and the gospel recounts how, like any other Jewish male child, he was circumcised on the octave day of his birth (today is the final day of the Christmas Octave).

The first reading (Numbers 6:22-27) consists of an instruction on the blessing to be given by the priests. Was it a similar blessing that Jesus and Mary received when she took him to the Temple to be circumcised? The second reading (Galatians 4:4-7) teaches us that it is through Christ in his humanity, Christ 'born of a woman, born subject to the Law', that God has given us the greatest of all blessings, a sharing in the divine life so that we are enabled to call upon him as 'Abba' (dear Father).

In the first part of the gospel (Luke 2:16-21), the shepherds visit the new-born Christ and worship him, and then go on their way blessing and praising God. The responsorial psalm is part of a thanksgiving prayer – Psalm 66 – taking up the theme of the shepherds, it blesses and praises the Lord. Originally it was intended as a thanksgiving for the harvest, indeed it may have been composed for a harvest festival such as the Feast of Tabernacles. Only part of it is used in today's Mass; the explicit reference to harvest is absent, and that is unfortunate because today is the feast of Mary's motherhood, and Jesus, the fruit of her womb, is surely the richest harvest this world has ever witnessed.

Prayerful Ponderings

'God, be gracious and bless us and let your face shed its light upon us.'

These words are an adaptation of the blessing which, according to Numbers 6:24-26, Aaron and his sons were to use when they blessed the people. It is a blessing which the priests had pronounced over and over again throughout Israel's history. But never was the whole world blessed so magnificently as it was through the Divine Motherhood of Mary, for her Son is God's graciousness, God's blessing, the radiant smile of God's face made visible.

'So will your ways be known upon earth and all nations learn your saving help.'

However, it quickly becomes clear that the blessing of the Saviour's birth is to be spread over the whole earth. The good news of Bethlehem is to be taken to all the nations so that everyone will become aware of the wonderful ways of God and of his readiness to offer 'saving help' to all who are ready to receive it.

'Let the nations be glad and exult for you rule the world with justice.'

We Christians, like the Jews before us, find joy in the 'rule' and kingship of our God, and our prayer is that his 'justice', his impartiality and fairness, may be experienced by our brothers and sisters everywhere.

'With fairness you rule the peoples, you guide the nations on earth.' It was always Israel's prayer that their earthly king would function as shepherd of his people: his task was not simply to 'rule', but also to 'guide'; power and strength were to merge with tenderness and concern for those in his care. In Jesus we find just such a king; his is 'a kingdom of truth and life, a kingdom of holiness and grace, a kingdom of justice, love and peace'.

'Let the peoples praise you, O God; let all the peoples praise you.' This psalm has links with two great Old Testament prophecies. The first is God's promise to Abraham that he will be blessed and then in his turn will be a blessing to all the families of the earth (Genesis 12:1-3). The second is the prophecy which emerges in Isaiah 40-55 that the salvation of Israel will be a revelation to all the nations that the Lord reigns and will lead them to praise him (for example 40:1-5; 45:21-25). In both cases Israel is the bridgehead by which God's blessing spreads throughout the world. It is through the Church, the 'sacrament' or effective sign of God's salvation, that the whole world is to be drawn to praise him.

'May God still give us his blessing till the ends of the earth revere him.' The responsorial psalm ends with this appeal that God will continue to favour us with such blessings that we in our turn may prove to be a blessing to 'the ends of the earth' – to everyone everywhere.

LET US PRAY: *Lord, we thank you for the harvest of blessings we have received from you, and above all for your dear Son Jesus, born of the Virgin Mary. We beg you to continue to bless us day by day so that we may bear witness to you unceasingly and others may thereby be drawn to you.*

Second Sunday
after Christmas

Psalm 147 was composed for the congregation of Jerusalem which, after long years in exile, had returned home and set about restoring city and Temple. The people were filled with a desire to praise God for they knew that the reversal of fortune was due to God's intervention: that it was he who enabled them to rejoice once more in Jerusalem, to experience peace, to enjoy plentiful harvests; and that it was he who blessed them with his words and decrees.

At Christmastide – Christmas Day is still only a short time ago – we too are encouraged to raise our voices in praise as we recall all the good things that have come our way, thanks to the birth and life of Jesus. He has 'pitched his tent among us' (see the first reading [Ecclesiasticus 24:1-2, 8-12] and the gospel [John 1:1-18]); he has destroyed our alienation from God, raising us to dizzy heights as the adopted children of God (see the second reading [Ephesians 1:3-6, 15-18]); and he has drawn us into the 'Jerusalem' of his Church.

Prayerful Ponderings

'The Word was made flesh, and lived among us.'
These words are not of course part of the psalm – they come from
St John's Gospel – but they are an admirable response to the psalm
when it is viewed through Christian eyes. Our supreme reason for
making this song of praise our own is that God has come to us in
the person of Jesus Christ: he, the Word, Almighty Son of God, has
taken upon himself our human condition and the consequences are
wonderful beyond anything we could imagine.

'O praise the Lord, Jerusalem! Zion, praise your God!'
In the psalms the word 'Jerusalem' does not always refer to the city
of that name; sometimes it means all the citizens, or even the whole
people of God. And today we, God's people, pray this psalm to
praise God for what he has done in building the 'new Jerusalem',
his Church (which is itself a foretaste of the new Jerusalem of
heaven), and for upholding it amidst all the eventualities of history.

**'He has strengthened the bars of your gates, he has blessed the
children within you.'**
When the exiles returned, they had to look to the defence of their
city; sturdy wooden bars ensured that when the city gates were
closed they were secure. Within that security the people could
again grow in numbers, after the terrible losses they had sustained.

Nonetheless, they saw within and above their activities the loving care of God for his people. As we pray this psalm we too thank God for the care he lavishes on his Church, ensuring that 'the gates of hell will not prevail against it' and blessing it in every age with new children in the sacrament of baptism.

'He established peace on your borders, he feeds you with finest wheat.'

This is another line which takes on richer meaning when applied to the Church, whose peace and essential unity God preserves despite scandals and set-backs and divisions. Above all, the Lord feeds us with 'finest wheat' – himself in the Holy Eucharist – and the first purpose of Holy Communion is to build up a common-union of love first with him and then with one another.

'He sends out his word to the earth and swiftly runs his command. He makes his word known to Jacob, to Israel his laws and decrees.'

The 'laws and decrees' given by God to his covenant people (Jacob/Israel) were seen as a revelation of his will and therefore as a precious gift. The distinguishing feature of this people was the fact that God had spoken to them, they had heard his word. And in the Church we rejoice in God's word, the Scriptures through which he reveals himself to us, and, above all, in his Word (with a capital letter) whose birthday we are now celebrating and whose teaching is our joy.

'He has not dealt thus with other nations; he has not taught them his decrees.'

Israel rejoiced in the singular gifts that God had bestowed upon them. It was only with the passage of time that they began to realise that God's gifts, in particular his revelation, were not just for them but for the whole human race. There is no excuse for us Christians, however, if we do not recognise the universal implications of our Lord's coming. His last word to his disciples was that they should go forth and teach all nations, baptising all who would believe and bringing them into the bosom of the Church.

LET US PRAY: *We thank and praise you, Lord, for the gifts that you have bestowed upon us so generously. We ask you to keep your family in your peace and continue to sustain us with the bread of the Eucharist that we may be filled with a sense of security and of hope.*

The Epiphany of the Lord

The Epiphany is one of the oldest Christian feasts. It is not only older than Christmas, but also has a deeper significance, for rather than celebrating simply the birth of Christ, it also celebrates the whole purpose of his incarnation – the 'epiphany', that is, the appearance or manifestation of God through his Son Jesus. And so it serves as a fitting end to the Christmas season.

Today's first reading (Isaiah 60:1-6) is full of optimism: the people will be brought back home from exile and Jerusalem, once restored, will manifest the Lord to all peoples, drawing them from darkness into glorious light. Paul takes up a similar theme (Ephesians 3:2-3, 5-6): the secret at the heart of Christianity is that all peoples, Jews and non-Jews alike, are called to be members of the one Body of which Jesus is the Head.

Today's gospel (Matthew 2:1-12) also bears witness to the universal character of the 'good news', for it tells of the visit of the Magi, probably practitioners in the occult arts, who come from far-away lands with gifts – it seems that the practice of gift-giving at Christmastide arose from this episode – for the new-born King.

The responsorial psalm, taken from Psalm 71, with the response 'All nations shall fall prostrate before you, O Lord', chimes in well with the other readings: the Messiah King will be worshipped by all peoples, he will be reverenced and plied with gifts even by kings from distant lands.

Prayerful Ponderings

'O God, give your judgement to the king, to a king's son your justice, that he may judge your people in justice and your poor in right judgement.'
In all probability this psalm was composed for the coronation of a Davidic king in Jerusalem, but it is a portrait so utopian that no one could ever live up to its incredible ideals except that Messianic king who was born in the humble setting of a stable. He, as we know, is not merely the 'king's son', but the Son of the King of kings. That is why he can be relied upon to reflect 'your justice', a justice worthy of God himself, and to show a special concern for the poor, for they are God's poor ('your poor').

'In his days justice shall flourish and peace till the moon fails. He shall rule from sea to sea, from the Great River to earth's bounds.'
His reign, bringing with it 'justice' and every kind of well-being (*shalom*), will endure for ever – even 'till the moon fails', as the psalmist quaintly puts it. Just as the King's reign is endless, so his realm is boundless, 'from sea to sea', an expression which may refer to the promised boundaries of the holy land, from 'the Great River' of the Euphrates to the sea of the Mediterranean, or to the ancient notion that the earth was like an island in the midst of waters, so that 'from sea to sea' would be equivalent to from east to west.

'The kings of Tarshish and the sea coasts shall pay him tribute. The kings of Sheba and Seba shall bring him gifts. Before him all kings shall fall prostrate, all nations shall serve him.'

Whatever the precise location of 'Tarshish and the sea coasts' – the reference is perhaps to Spain – the expression is certainly meant to underline the fact that it is from the ends of the earth that kings come to acknowledge the King. There seems little doubt that in his account of the Magi's visit, Matthew had in mind the psalmist's reference to gift-bearing 'kings of Sheba and Seba'. A queen of Sheba once arrived in Jerusalem laden with gifts for King Solomon (1 Kings 10), but there is 'a greater than Solomon here', though born in a lowly stable.

'For he shall save the poor when they cry and the needy who are helpless. He will have pity on the weak and save the lives of the poor.'

Once more it is made clear that the long-awaited King will be full of compassion; he will have a special concern for 'the poor', 'the needy' and 'the weak'; indeed, he will have practical experience of the lot of the poor.

LET US PRAY: *On this day of Christmastide, we give thanks to you, Lord, for drawing us into the kingdom of your Son and enabling us to see in him the most perfect revelation of yourself. Like the Magi, may we bow low before him, offering the precious gifts of our faith, our hope and our love.*

The Baptism of the Lord

If, as scholars believe, Psalm 28, today's psalm, was once a Canaanite hymn in honour of the storm god who brought new life and fertility to the crops, then it is one of the oldest psalms in the Psalter. It has been skilfully adapted for use in the service of Israel's God (his name, 'Yahweh', appears no fewer than 18 times in this short psalm). It's a hymn of praise to his power and glory, which the psalmist sees displayed in a thunderstorm.

In the old dispensation God's glory is glimpsed in the wonders of nature; in the new it is revealed supremely in Jesus of Nazareth whose mighty deeds are 'signs' that he shares in the divine majesty: to believe in him is already to see his glory (John 1:14); in his crucifixion he is revealed as 'the Lord of glory' (1 Corinthians 2:8).

The use of this psalm in today's liturgy suggests a comparison between on the one hand the mighty storm, which whips up the waters of the sea while it heralds God's complete mastery of nature, and on the other the quiet unpretentious baptism of Jesus in the waters of the river Jordan (Matthew 3:13-17). In the thunderstorm the 'voice' of the Lord is heard announcing: 'This is my universe'; in the baptism the voice of the Father is heard proclaiming: 'This is my Son, the Beloved; my favour rests on him.' The young man emerging from the Jordan is both Son of God and Lord of creation.

But today's first reading (Isaiah 42:1-4, 6-7) reveals that this Beloved Son of the mighty God is also God's Servant. In contrast to the thundering voice in today's psalm, his voice will never be raised and he will never 'break the crushed reed'. Nonetheless, he is the binding covenant between God and the people and his power is so great that he will 'open the eyes of the blind' and 'free captives'. As St Peter expresses it (Acts 10:34-38), God anointed Jesus 'with the Holy Spirit' so that he 'went about doing good' and has brought to us all 'the good news of peace'.

Prayerful Ponderings

'O give the Lord you sons of God, give the Lord glory and power; give the Lord the glory of his name.'
Originally the 'sons of God' were the offspring of the pagan gods but now they are 'angels', like the mighty seraphim whom Isaiah saw worshipping God in the Temple (Isaiah 6:2-6). The threefold repetition of the phrase 'give the Lord' helps to create a sense of mounting wonder and excitement: because of 'the glory of his name' – the very nature of who he is – they are called upon to worship him.

'Adore the Lord in his holy court.'
In this extraordinary hymn, the summons to praise goes out first not to human beings but to angelic ones; it is a question not of earthly but of heavenly worship, worship 'in his holy court'. Scripture reminds us that all earthly worship is only 'a model or reflection of the heavenly realities' (Hebrews 8:5), a theme taken up by the Vatican Council: 'in the earthly liturgy we take part in a foretaste of that heavenly liturgy which is celebrated in the holy city [of heaven]... where Christ is sitting at the right hand of God' (Sacred Liturgy §8).

'The Lord's voice resounding on the waters, the Lord on the immensity of waters; the voice of the Lord, full of power, the voice of the Lord, full of splendour.'

At this point there begins a vivid description of a thunderstorm which resounds on the waters of the Mediterranean, then rolls inland, runs down the land and eventually rumbles away into the distant desert wastes. The responsorial psalm omits verses 5 to 9; but today you need to read them for yourself in your Bible if you are to get the impact of this psalm: it tells of huge cedars shattered, the very mountains shaken, forests stripped bare; together with the dull roll of the thunder there are flashes of lightning. It all adds up to what has been described as God's own 'Son et Lumière' (his sound and light display) – a striking image of his power and majesty.

'The God of glory thunders. In his temple they all cry: "Glory!"'
This verse is perhaps the climax of the psalm, for in response to the thundering of 'the God of glory' there comes the answering call of recognition from God's people, as they cry: 'Glory!' For them the storm is not a riotous outbreak of meaningless forces but the sound of 'God's voice': to those who have eyes to see and heart to understand, God is 'speaking' through the storm.

'The Lord sat enthroned over the flood; the Lord sits as king for ever.'
The Lord revealed in the storm is a king: he sits on his throne above the 'flood', the waters that surround the earth, and his kingship lasts for ever. Shortly after his baptism, Jesus announced that he had come to proclaim and launch the 'kingdom of heaven', the reign of God on this earth.

'The Lord will bless his people with peace.'
This final line serves as the response to each verse. Just as the praise which began in heaven is taken up on earth, so the 'Glory to God'

of verse 1 becomes the 'peace on earth' of the final verse: the hymn of Bethlehem (Luke 2:14) could equally well have been spoken over the Jordan when Jesus was baptised.

LET US PRAY: *Lord God, at our baptism your voice sounded over the waters, proclaiming us to be your beloved children; help us to live lives worthy of our calling so that we, like your servants in heaven, may give you glory.*

LENT

*By
his sufferings
shall
my servant
justify
many*

LENT

*'The season of Lent is a
preparation for the celebration of
Easter. The liturgy prepares the
catechumens for the celebration of
the paschal mystery...
it also prepares the faithful who
recall their baptism and do penance
in preparation for Easter'*
(General Norms for the Liturgical Year §27)

First Sunday of Lent

As we move into the graced season of Lent, today's first reading (Genesis 2:7-9; 3:1-7) recalls how our first parents sinned; the second (Romans 5:12-19) tells how the saga of sin continued in the world but also proclaims the wonderful good news that through one man life and justification have been made available to all; and, finally, the gospel (Matthew 4:1-11) shows how that one man, Jesus Christ, severely tempted though he was, remained faithful to his Father and resolute in resisting the devil's temptations.

Early in the Church's history, probably by the fifth century at the latest, seven psalms had been recognised as prayers of penitence, particularly suitable for the Lenten season. They came to be known as 'the penitential psalms'. However, the best known within that group is undoubtedly Psalm 50 and so traditionally it has been regarded as the most appropriate psalm to introduce the Lenten season. Though it is the prayer of an individual, the response − 'Have mercy on us, O Lord, for we have sinned' − makes it clear that sin involves the whole people of God. In fact the Hebrews never saw sin as a purely personal matter, but as an evil which affected the community.

Prayerful Ponderings

'Have mercy on me, God, in your kindness. In your compassion blot out my offence.'

The Hebrews had no fewer than three words for sin. The first, which appears in this verse, means not so much 'my offence' as 'my rebellion'; every sin is an act of rebellion, an act which says in deed: 'I will not serve'. With the psalmist we beg God to show his loving kindness and his mother-like compassion (in Hebrew the word for 'compassion' is closely linked with that for 'womb') by blotting out our rebellious behaviour.

'O wash me more and more from my guilt and cleanse me from my sin.'

This verse brings us the two words 'guilt' and 'sin'. The former might be translated 'crookedness', indicating that through sin we become malformed, displeasing in God's sight; and the latter suggests 'missing the mark', like an arrow that fails to hit its target, and so reminds us of another aspect of sin: it prevents us from reaching our true end. We pray that we may be washed thoroughly, like the laundering of a dirty garment, until we are truly cleansed.

'My offences truly I know them; my sin is always before me. Against you, you alone, have I sinned; what is evil in your sight I have done.'

There's something refreshing in this lowly admission of guilt. No excuses offered, simply the humble acknowledgement that 'I have sinned' – it's not been a question simply of a slip-up or a shortcoming or a weakness but of downright sin – and the recognition of what sin is and, therefore, of who is offended by it ('evil in your sight'). At the same time, we need to remember that, from an Old Testament, and indeed a Christian, point of view, it is inconceivable that there can be any sin, however secret, which besides affecting our relationship with God does not also injure others.

'A pure heart create me for me, O God, put a steadfast spirit within me.'
What is required amounts to a re-creation of our inmost being, and only God can do that; indeed in the language of the Old Testament the word 'create' is used only in reference to God's activity. And if it is he alone who can create, it is also he alone who can place within us 'a steadfast spirit', a mind and will set unwaveringly towards God and his will.

'Do not cast me away from your presence, nor deprive me of your holy spirit.'
Whatever happens, may we not suffer the loss of God's presence (for that would indeed mean hell). Furthermore, the psalmist prays that he may not lose 'your holy spirit'. The reference is probably to the spirit (or breath) of life; but we pray that we may not forfeit the Holy Spirit, 'best gift of God above' and pledge of eternal glory.

'Give me again the joy of your help; with a spirit of fervour sustain me. O Lord, open my lips and my mouth shall declare your praise.'

A final plea that we may experience the joy that comes from knowing that God is helping us, that our enthusiasm in his service may be sustained and that we may be enabled gladly to open our mouths and hearts in his praise.

LET US PRAY: *Lord, as we begin our Lenten journey, we pray that we may have the humility to acknowledge the sin in our lives, the wisdom to repent and then the grace and joy of singing the praises of your Son, through whose paschal mystery we have become your own sons and daughters.*

Second Sunday of Lent

As we reach this second Sunday in Lent the liturgy invites us to recall the beginning of the story of our salvation – God's astonishing call to Abraham and Abraham's generous response (Genesis 12:1-4). Asked to leave a stable home and become a wandering nomad, with no strong son to protect him and with only vague promises of what the future will bring, Abraham, already an old man, sets out, trusting in the Lord. Little wonder that the first Eucharistic Prayer describes him as 'our father in faith', the one whose faith and trust in the Lord serve as an example for all who follow in his footsteps, all who belong to the family of faith.

In his letter to Timothy (2 Timothy 1:8-10) St Paul makes it clear that the God who called Abraham has also 'called us'. The call is to holiness, but a holiness not of our making – 'not because of anything we ourselves have done' – but of God's making – 'by his own grace'. Like Abraham, we too must learn to live trusting in God's grace, his steadfast faithfulness.

It is a trust exemplified supremely in the life of Jesus. Today's gospel (Matthew 17:1-9) shows him on the mountain top, radiant with light and acknowledged as God's own 'beloved Son'; yet before long he will be overwhelmed with suffering. It may well be that one of the purposes of his transfiguration is to strengthen the faith of the three disciples who, in a few months' time, will see him in agony in the garden. Then they will know that he too must walk the way of trial and of boundless trust. He will cry out in anguish: 'My God, my God, why have you forsaken me?'; but his final words will be filled with confidence: 'Father, into your hands I commend my spirit.'

The responsorial psalm, which comes in the main from the second half of Psalm 32, is a powerful encouragement to put our trust in God whose abiding love will never fail us.

Prayerful Ponderings

'The word of the Lord is faithful and all his works to be trusted.'
This psalm, which begins as a call to praise God, to worship him
with music and song, goes on to explain why he is deserving of
worship. First of all because his 'word is faithful'; one can depend
upon it with utter confidence, as Abraham discovered long ago. It
is never an empty word; that is why what the Lord does ('all his
works') matches what he says; his work and his word are of a piece
and always worthy of our trust.

'The Lord loves justice and right and fills the earth with his love.'
The Lord is deserving of praise because, along with the faithfulness
of his words and actions, go uprightness and justice in all that he
does. But above all there is 'his love'. The Hebrew word *hesed*, one
of the key words of the Bible, may be translated in different ways.
Fundamentally, it expresses the Lord's faithfulness to the special
relationship, the covenant, which binds him to his people. So it can
mean loving kindness, goodness or, quite simply, steadfast love. And
the psalmist assures us that the whole of creation is filled with, is
the expression of, that steadfast love.

'The Lord looks on those who revere him, on those who hope
in his love, to rescue their souls from death, to keep them alive
in famine.'

Having spoken of his creative word and of his eternal plans – though this does not appear in the section of Psalm 32 which makes up today's responsorial psalm – the psalmist goes on to reflect upon God's loving gaze, which is turned with limitless compassion towards those who reverence him, who put their trust in 'his love'. He will be with them in every critical moment, such as when life is threatened or the land is visited by famine.

'Our soul is waiting for the Lord. The Lord is our help and our shield.'
And so we wait upon the Lord, ready, like Abraham and still more like our beloved Lord, to follow wherever the Father may lead, for we know that he is our sure source of 'help'; in every eventuality we can picture him with his strong arms folded about us like a protective 'shield'.

'May your love be upon us, O Lord, as we place all our hope in you.'
A final plea that his *hesed*, his steadfast love, may be 'upon us', and indeed upon all who place their trust in him.

LET US PRAY: *Lord, with Abraham, our father in faith, and with Jesus, our brother, we pray that your loving kindness may be with us throughout our lives, and especially now as we pursue our Lenten journey.*

Third Sunday of Lent

After the call of Abraham, referred to in last week's readings, one of the next major events in Israel's history was the Exodus. An echo of that event is caught in today's first reading (Exodus 17:3-7) which describes what happened after the deliverance from Egypt: as they wander through the desert, the people begin to 'murmur' against God, for they fear that having been led by Moses into the wilderness they will now die there of thirst; they harden their hearts in lack of trust. After appealing to God, Moses is able to respond to their needs but the place where the event took place is for ever to be known as the place of 'murmuring'.

Today's psalm, Psalm 94, is based in part upon the incident recorded in the first reading; its response runs as follows: 'O that today you would listen to his voice: "Harden not your hearts." ' We pray that we may not follow the example of our ancestors by losing confidence in God, by hardening our hearts in lack of trust.

In his letter to the Romans (5:1-2, 5-8) Paul speaks of an outpouring of God which is even more precious than that of water – 'the love of God [that] has been poured into our hearts by the Holy Spirit which has been given us'.

The long but beautiful gospel (John 4:5-42) shows Jesus himself longing for water to slake his thirst after he has been trudging through desert places. He asks the Samaritan woman to give him a drink, assuring her that he himself has a gift to offer her, the gift of 'living water', water 'welling up to eternal life'. She proves to be a woman who does not harden her heart but listens carefully to all that Jesus has to say to her and ends up not only by acknowledging him as Saviour but also by bringing that good news to her fellow citizens.

Prayerful Ponderings

'Come, ring out our joy to the Lord; hail the rock who saves us.'
The opening words of the psalm suggest that a group of people, perhaps recently arrived from the countryside, are about to enter the Temple. A priest, or some other temple official, calls out to them, inviting them to join him in worship: 'Come,' he cries, 'ring out our joy to the Lord', praise him, greet him, our rescuer who is as sure and dependable as a 'rock'.

'Let us come before him, giving thanks, with songs let us hail the Lord.'
There's to be praise and worship, but also thanksgiving. All are invited to raise their voice in song – using perhaps some of the thanksgiving psalms that appear in the Psalter. It's encouraging to note that from earliest times true worshippers of God have recognised that genuine prayer is not simply a matter of making requests: it always has room for gratitude.

'Come in; let us bow and bend low; let us kneel before the God who made us for he is our God and we the people who belong to his pasture, the flock that is led by his hand.'
Again the cry goes up, 'Come, let us go in', and that is followed by further directions: to 'bow' down, to 'bend low', to go down reverently on the knees; actions as well as words are to be used to express the depth of worship. And all this because we are God's own creation, it is he 'who

made us'. We stand in a special relationship with him: he is 'our God' or, to change the metaphor, he is our shepherd, always full of solicitude for his flock, caring for us with 'his [own] hand'.

'O that today you would listen to his voice!'

Given what has just been said, it would be a form of madness if we were not to 'listen to his voice'. As the letter to the Hebrews reminds us (see 3:7-19), the 'today' of this psalm is the present opportunity – this season of Lent – for it is now, if we would but listen, that the Lord is speaking to us. However, he speaks to us not only through the Scriptures but also through the people we meet and the events of our daily lives. Only if we are attentive to his voice will we successfully negotiate our desert journeying through this world and eventually reach the Promised Land.

'Harden not your hearts as at Meribah, as on that day at Massah in the desert when your fathers put me to the test; when they tried me, though they saw my work.'

Our response to his voice is to be boundless trust in the 'rock of our salvation'. The two place names, 'Meribah' (dispute) and 'Massah' (testing), serve as a summary of the cynical spirit of the Israelites during their desert journey (see the first reading). Though they had had abundant evidence of his activity, his 'work', in the miracle of the Exodus, yet they were prepared to put him to the test; they 'tried him' by raising the question: 'Is the Lord among us or not?' We are urged not to follow that unsavoury example.

LET US PRAY: *Lord, this season of Lent can sometimes seem a hard, desert-like experience. Help us not to lose heart, above all not to lose confidence in you but rather to listen with ever greater keenness for your voice.*

Fourth Sunday of Lent

The first reading on each of the previous two Sundays has focused in turn upon Abraham and Moses. This week (1 Samuel 16:1, 6-7, 10-13) it focuses upon the third outstanding personage in Israel's history – David. The prophet Samuel singled out the youthful and inexperienced David, who worked in the fields as a shepherd, to become king of Israel in preference to any of his seven older and apparently more impressive-looking brothers; but then, as the reading explains, 'man looks at appearances but the Lord looks at the heart'.

If, as popular tradition has it, David was author of Psalm 22, today's responsorial psalm, he leaves us in no doubt that, though he may be king, yet the real Shepherd-King of Israel is none other than God himself.

The assurance that even 'in the valley of darkness' there is nothing to fear, gives the psalm a link with the wonderful gospel of this Sunday (John 9:1-41), which tells how a man born blind was given sight by Jesus. Not only does he gain his sight, but, little by little, he also gains such insight that he comes to recognise Jesus as the Saviour. Meanwhile, the proud Pharisees go deeper and deeper into darkness as they reject the Light of the World. The second reading (Ephesians 5:8-14) is also concerned with light as it exhorts Christians to live as children of light because, through baptism, they have been enlightened by Jesus.

It is worth noting that in parishes that follow the rite of Christian initiation (RCIA), this is the Sunday when special prayers are said that God will 'enable them [the Christians-to-be] to pass from darkness to light and, delivered from the prince of darkness, to live always as children of the light'. Psalm 22, as we shall see, has much to offer to those who are travelling towards baptism, as well as those of us who during these Lenten days are preparing for a renewal of baptismal promises.

Prayerful Ponderings

'The Lord is my shepherd; there is nothing I shall want. Fresh and green are the pastures where he gives me repose.'
To be baptised is to have entered into a special relationship with the Lord. He becomes 'my' shepherd, one who has a personal interest in me. In biblical times, the shepherd lived with his sheep and meant everything to them. He was their guide, their protector, their physician. That is how the Lord had treated his people, especially during their days in the desert.

For those who are baptised, as for those preparing for baptism, there is enormous comfort in the fact that the Lord is 'the shepherd and guardian' of our souls (1 Peter 2:25); we can afford to be at rest in his safe keeping.

'Near restful waters he leads me, to revive my drooping spirit. He guides me along the right path; he is true to his name.'
One of the shepherd's most important tasks was to lead his flock to places where they could be watered: in desert lands it is water that makes the difference between life and death. In today's reading of this psalm we recall that our Divine Shepherd has brought us to the life-giving waters of baptism, and now, 'true to his name' as Shepherd, 'he guides along the right path' so that we may walk worthily as the sons and daughters of God.

'If I should walk in the valley of darkness no evil would I fear. You are there with your crook and your staff; with these you give me comfort.'
In 1975 Sheila Cassidy, then working as a doctor in Chile, was arrested by secret police for offering medical help to a wounded revolutionary.

She has described how while being interrogated under torture she 'knew' that God was there with her, not intervening to put an end to the ghastly suffering yet nonetheless leaving her convinced of his love for her. In other 'valleys of darkness', even though suffering is not eliminated, there is 'comfort' and reassurance to be found in the conviction that 'you are there'. No longer is God simply spoken of as 'he', but rather addressed familiarly, and prayerfully, as 'you'.

'You have prepared a banquet for me in the sight of my foes. My head you have anointed with oil; my cup is overflowing.'
A change of metaphor! The Shepherd has become the Host, and a most generous one: 'a banquet' awaits the guests, there is 'oil' for their anointing and a 'cup' full to overflowing. As we hear of the generous provision, we cannot but think of the eucharistic table with its cup of salvation and the anointing with the Spirit that new Christians receive immediately after their baptism.

'Surely goodness and kindness shall follow me all the days of my life. In the Lord's own house shall I dwell for ever and ever.'
Awareness of this outpouring of divine favours leads to a fundamental Christian optimism: we are confident that the Lord will continue what he has begun; his 'goodness and kindness' will follow us our whole life through and we look forward, beyond death, to enjoying his company for ever in 'the Lord's own house', for our Good Shepherd has gone before us 'to prepare a place' (John 14:2-4) for us.

LET US PRAY: *As your Son gave sight to the blind man, Lord, may you give sight to the eyes of our hearts that we may appreciate the wonder of our baptism and the benefits that flow from it.*

Fifth Sunday of Lent

Lent is driving towards its climax in Passiontide and the readings of today's Mass centre upon the Lord as giver of life: it is through Christ's death and resurrection that the new life will become available to us.

The prophet Ezekiel (Ezekiel 37:12-14) encourages his fellow exiles with the assurance that God will bring them back to life by restoring them to their own land; it will be as if they had been raised from the grave.

The gospel account (John 11:1-45) is more than 'as if': it is a record of Jesus' actual raising from the grave of his friend Lazarus, though he had been dead for four days and, according to his sister, would already have the smell of putrefaction about him. However, this most stupendous of miracles was a 'sign' of something even greater − a sign that Jesus is 'the resurrection and the life' and that soon, through his paschal mystery, he will be a source of resurrection and eternal life for all who believe in him.

The response to today's psalm, Psalm 129, helps to reinforce the truth that our trust in God must be unlimited because 'mercy', loving faithfulness, and 'fullness of redemption' are what we can expect at the hands of the Lord.

Similarly, Paul (Romans 8:8-11) boldly affirms that 'if the Spirit of him who raised Jesus from the dead is living in you, then he… will give life to your own mortal bodies…'

Prayerful Ponderings

**'Out of the depths I cry to you, O Lord, Lord hear my voice!
O let your ears be attentive to the voice of my pleading.'**
Whatever 'the depths' in which we find ourselves – whether it be the
depths of sin, or of anxiety, or of suffering, or even of death itself – the
message of this psalm is that we have only to 'cry' to the Lord. The
expressions the psalmist uses might seem to suggest that the cry has to
be loud if the Lord is to hear, that in fact the Lord is rather hard of
hearing. However, they are simply a poetical way of encouraging us
to pray with sincerity. As for the Lord, there is not the slightest danger
that he will not be 'attentive' to our pleas. If we dare put it this way,
he is all ears where we, his beloved children, are concerned.

**'If you, O Lord, should mark our guilt, Lord, who would survive?
But with you is found forgiveness: for this we revere you.'**
The most terrible 'depths' of all is sin. It has been said that if we
each had to carry a bill-board listing the full record of our sins,
none of us would venture out of doors, for shame. But sin is an
offence against God; it brings not merely shame but guilt, for it is
rebellion of the creature against the creator. If the Lord were to
'mark' our sins, chalk them up on his slate and hold them against
us, there wouldn't be a chance for any of us. But, proclaims the
psalmist in a great act of faith, that is precisely what the Lord does
not do: with him is found 'forgiveness' and for that reason especially
'we revere' him, stand in awe of his generosity. It was while listening

to the words of this verse being sung in St Paul's Cathedral that John Wesley felt that his heart was 'strangely warmed': it was the first step on his way to conversion.

'My soul is waiting for the Lord, I count on his word. My soul is longing for the Lord more than watchman for daybreak. (Let the watchman count on daybreak and Israel on the Lord.)'
In the strength of this act of faith, the psalmist knows that he can 'count on [the Lord's] word' of forgiveness, and so pictures himself waiting for the Lord, 'longing' for his coming; and, despite weariness, eager and confident that the Lord will come – as utterly sure of it as a night watchman is sure of tomorrow's dawn. The psalm urges 'Israel', the people of God – and today all of us who pray this psalm – to share the same confident expectation.

'Because with the Lord there is mercy and fullness of redemption, Israel indeed he will redeem from all its iniquity.'
And finally the reasons for confidence are once again spelt out clearly: first, the Lord's boundless 'mercy' (*hesed*), his unconditional love, and secondly the 'fullness' of his saving work, which is universal in scope, reaching out to every person, and powerful enough to bring life, eternal life, out of death. As Paul was later to say: 'we have our hope set on the living God, who is the Saviour of all people' (1 Timothy 4:10).

LET US PRAY: *O God, on this Lenten Sunday, as we recall the mercy and fullness of redemption revealed to us through Jesus your Son, we are emboldened to cry out with confidence and beg you to draw us 'out of the depths', above all the depths of our sinfulness.*

Passion Sunday

It is hardly surprising that the verses of Psalm 21 which feature in the Mass of Passion Sunday (Palm Sunday) also appear in Masses during Holy Week: they offer us vivid reminders of our Lord's sufferings as well as the first glimmers of his Easter glory.

The psalm itself might have been composed for the mysterious 'disciple' – his identity is not revealed – whom we meet in the passage from Isaiah (50:4-7). There are three similar passages in the second section of Isaiah and all four are commonly referred to as 'Servant Songs', for they speak of a disciple who is the utterly faithful servant of the Lord, who suffers much without offering resistance and whose sufferings bring light and life to his people.

A key to the interpretation of the 'disciple' is to be found in St Paul's wonderful hymn in his letter to the Philippians (2:6-11), where Jesus is presented as one who though divine was the obedient servant of the Father and 'emptied himself' even to death on a cross, and so it is that he has been exalted and is now recognised by all as Lord.

Finally, today's gospel (Matthew 26:14-27:66) seems to bring all the above together – the words of the prophet, the hymn of the apostle and, in particular, the song of the psalmist, 'this magnificent Old Testament prayer' as it has been called. In fact virtually all the verses of Psalm 21 which appear in today's Mass were used by Matthew and the other gospel writers when they came to draw up their respective passion narratives.

Prayerful Ponderings

'My God, my God, why have you forsaken me?'
These words, the response for today's psalm, are taken from the opening verse of Psalm 21. They suggest that the psalm is peculiarly relevant to the passion story, for, according to Matthew (27:46), they were upon Jesus' lips as he hung upon the cross, a terrible cry of dereliction, as though he felt himself alienated even from his beloved Abba (dear Father). It is a cry which re-echoes the anguished 'Why?' of all men and women who are bewildered by their suffering. It is a cry which helps us to appreciate how completely our Saviour has 'emptied himself' for our sakes. Indeed St Paul says that he 'became a curse for us' (Galatians 3:13).

'All who see me deride me. They curl their lips, they toss their heads. "He trusted in the Lord, let him save him; let him release him if this is his friend."'
The early verses of the psalm depict the sufferer, now placing his complete trust in God, now complaining that God does not respond. He gazes down upon the upturned faces that surround him. He has become an object of derision to those who conspired to bring about his death; he notes the cynical curling of 'their lips', the dismissive 'toss [of] their heads'; he hears the almost unbearable taunt: if you really did trust in God, really were his friend, then he would surely intervene on your behalf (see Matthew 27:43-44). But God remains silent. The passion continues.

'Many dogs have surrounded me, a band of the wicked beset me. They tear holes in my hands and my feet. I can count every one of my bones.'

The middle section of the psalm reads like a nightmare: enemies appear in the guise of salivating 'dogs' and other fearful animals, waiting to tear him to pieces. Already 'hands' and 'feet' have been split open to provide a pathway for the nails of crucifixion. He has become so disfigured and emaciated that as his glance runs down his body he can count his very 'bones', protruding through the flesh.

'They divide my clothing among them. They cast lots for my robe. O Lord, do not leave me alone, my strength, make haste to help me!'

A particularly painful aspect of his suffering is the shame and humiliation it brings. For this most noble and sensitive of men, how degrading to be stripped naked! But that is of no concern to the executioners, who are intent only upon seizing his 'robe', their bonus for a job well done. It is at this moment that the victim calls out once again to the Lord; even now he begs him 'do not leave me alone', even now he has confidence enough to call upon him as 'my strength' and to plead with him to 'make haste to help me'.

'I will tell of your name to my brethren and praise you where they are assembled. "You who fear the Lord give him praise; all sons of Jacob, give him glory. Revere him, Israel's sons."'

The third part of the psalm, from which this verse is taken, is the most unexpected part of all. The Suffering Servant has become the Conquering Victor: in the midst of his anguish, he confidently asserts that he will proclaim God's goodness wherever 'my brethren... are assembled'. It is difficult to listen to these words and not to think of the glory of the resurrection. Psalm 21 is not simply a cry of anguish but ultimately a hymn of praise to God who brings victory out of defeat. He is the God whom we shall 'fear' (reverence) and 'praise' and glorify as Good Friday gives way to Easter Sunday.

LET US PRAY: *Lord God, we give you thanks for the death and resurrection of your Son Jesus, for in these events we see the clearest proof of your undying love for us. Help us to live lives worthy of such love.*

EASTERTIDE

*This
is the day
which was made
by the Lord:
let us
rejoice*

EASTERTIDE

*'The fifty days from Easter Sunday
to Pentecost are celebrated as one feast day,
sometimes called "the great Sunday"'*
(General Norms for the Liturgical Year §12)

Easter Sunday

Today we arrive at the first of the Church's feast days and the pinnacle of the Church's liturgical year, the joyful celebration of the resurrection of our Lord Jesus Christ.

The gospel records (John 20:1-9) how the disciples Peter and John slowly came to the realisation that their Master had truly risen. Up to the moment when they stood in the empty tomb and gazed down upon linen cloths, no longer shrouding his body but lying discarded on the ground, they had simply 'failed to understand... that he must rise from the dead'.

However, as the first reading (Acts 10:34, 37-43) indicates, Peter was later able to proclaim not simply that God had 'raised [Jesus] to life' but that he and the other disciples had actually 'eaten and drunk with him after his resurrection from the dead'.

Each of the alternative second readings – the one taken from Colossians (3:1-4), the other from 1 Corinthians (5:6-8) – draws practical conclusions for all who, through baptism, share in the resurrection. Their new 'life... is hidden with Christ in God', and therefore their thoughts must no longer be anchored to this earth, they must rid themselves of 'the old yeast', the old way of life.

And finally all is brought together in Psalm 117, THE Easter psalm above all others. The verses for today's Mass are identical with those used at the Vigil Mass; and there will be many reminders of the psalm throughout the Easter season.

Prayerful Ponderings

'This day was made by the Lord; we rejoice and are glad.'
This sentence, which actually belongs to a later verse in Psalm 117, not only serves as the response to the psalm but also helps to set the tone for today's great feast. In fact it will be used for the Alleluia verse every day throughout the Easter Octave. Again and again we confess that this astounding day, which sees the resurrection of Jesus from the tomb, is the work of God himself. Only he could have brought it about, only he could even have envisaged such a wonder. And we, who only a few days ago were lamenting the death of Jesus, now find ourselves rejoicing and filled with gladness.

'Give thanks to the Lord for he is good, for his love has no end. Let the sons of Israel say: "His love has no end."'
This is the opening verse of the psalm; its first sentence serves also as the psalm's conclusion. This bracketing of the hymn with a call to give thanks not only indicates the nature of the psalm (a thanksgiving) but also suggests that it was originally used in a communal setting. Perhaps it was the occasion of an important individual's solemn entering of the Temple to express his gratitude, perhaps a king returning successfully from battle. But of course on this day of the Lord's own making, we think of the King of kings who by his resurrection has triumphed over every evil force that threatens human happiness. We think and we give thanks, for we know that Easter Sunday provides the clinching proof

of the goodness of our God and of his endless loving mercy. In the psalm all 'the sons of Israel', the whole people, are invited to take up the cry that 'his love has no end'. Today, for even more powerful reasons than Israel's, we are called to give thanks for God's undying love.

'The Lord's right hand has triumphed; his right hand raised me up. I shall not die, I shall live and recount his deeds.'
In the second section of the psalm, the singer speaks of being caught up in a terrible plight and then of the way in which defeat was turned into victory. Only the strong 'right hand' of God, a symbol of his power, could have turned the catastrophe of Good Friday into the triumph of Easter Sunday; it was that hand that 'raised... up' the crucified Christ. And, as St Paul says, 'Christ, having died, dies now no more, death shall no more have power over him' (Romans 6:9). The Risen Christ will never again face death; he lives for ever to 'recount [God's mighty] deeds'.

'The stone which the builders rejected has become the corner stone. This is the work of the Lord, a marvel in our eyes.'
And finally a wonderful word-picture highlights the incredible contrast between Jesus, disowned and crucified, and Jesus ablaze with resurrection glory. On Good Friday he, God's chosen stone, had been 'rejected' by the 'builders' (the leaders of the people), who regarded him as surplus to their requirements. But on Easter Sunday it becomes clear that God has vindicated the rejected stone, making him 'the corner stone' or keystone of a new structure, the new people of God. It's fascinating to see how naturally this metaphor of the discarded stone was used in the early Church in reference to Jesus' death and resurrection (Acts 4:11).

LET US PRAY: *Lord God, we are your Easter people; in the resurrection of your Son we 'have been brought back to true life'; and so we pray that, in the power of the Spirit, we may be renewed in mind and heart.*

Second Sunday of Easter

The rejoicing of Easter continues. Every Sunday is a 'little Easter', a celebration of the Lord's resurrection, but that is peculiarly so of the Sundays of Paschaltide.

In what may well have been a baptismal homily, St Peter (1 Peter 1:3-9) recalls that 'by raising Jesus Christ from the dead', the Father has given us 'a new birth as his sons [and daughters]', as well as the promise of an eternal inheritance and a faith 'more precious than gold'. Sufferings may come our way, but nothing can dampen the joy and love that comes from faith.

The first reading (Acts 2:42-47) shows how effectively Easter faith fashioned the first Christians so that they all acknowledged 'the teaching of the apostles', were united in a single 'brotherhood', found nourishment in 'the breaking of bread' (the Eucharist) and were committed to 'prayers' in common.

Today's gospel (John 20:19-31) recounts the events of the first Sunday after Easter Day. Thomas had been absent when the Risen Lord appeared to the other disciples and gave them the resurrection gift of peace; but now, a week later, Thomas also is granted an appearance of the Lord. It elicits from him the magnificent confession: 'My Lord and my God', and leads Jesus to assure us that the truly blessed ones are those (like ourselves) 'who have not seen and yet believe'.

Predictably, the responsorial psalm is again taken from Psalm 117. We have seen that originally it may have been associated with a king; we use it of *the* King, our Risen Lord.

Prayerful Ponderings

'Give thanks to the Lord for he is good, for his love has no end.' Today's response is taken from the opening words of the psalm. However, there is an alternative: the psalmist's words may be replaced by a triple 'Alleluia!' In either case the sense is much the same: praise and glory and thanksgiving be to our God and to his Son, risen from the dead, for their love which 'has no end'.

'Let the sons of Israel say: "His love has no end." Let the sons of Aaron say: "His love has no end." Let those who fear the Lord say: "His love has no end."'
This opening litany calls upon all the people to acknowledge that 'his love has no end'. First, the invitation goes out to 'the sons of Israel', the people in general; next to 'the sons of Aaron', the priests; then to 'those who fear the Lord', possibly those who believe in God though they do not belong to the Jewish community. But, finally, on this day the invitation is addressed to us; we too are encouraged to join in the chorus of grateful praise for God's *hesed*, his ever-faithful love.

'I was thrust, thrust down and falling but the Lord was my helper. The Lord is my strength and my song; he was my saviour.' It should be difficult for us to read this part of the psalm, where the king tells of the grim struggle he has had and how the Lord came to his help, without our thinking of all that Jesus has been through and how his Abba, dear Father, rescued him on Easter Day. What a blessing when we come to discover in our own lives that the Lord is our 'strength', our 'song' of joy, our 'saviour'.

'There are shouts of joy and victory in the tents of the just.'
The whole assembly takes up the song of God's victorious intervention. If in days gone by the people joined in a communal 'shout of joy and victory' when their king returned triumphant and told the story of his adventure, how much more readily we should hail our King on this his victory day.

'The stone which the builders rejected has become the corner stone. This is the work of the Lord, a marvel in our eyes. This day was made by the Lord; we rejoice and are glad.'
Once more the reversal of fortune between Good Friday and Easter Sunday is vividly presented under the metaphor of a stone 'rejected' by the builders as of no consequence but later singled out as the all-important 'corner stone'. Significantly, Jesus himself had appealed to this very verse to indicate how the leaders of the people would cast him aside (Matthew 21:42). And once again there is the acknowledgement that this is 'a marvel' which only the Lord could have achieved. Hence, this day is of the Lord's own making or, as we simply say, it is the Lord's day: for us, as for Christians down through the ages, a day of rejoicing and gladness.

LET US PRAY: *Loving Father, we thank you for the gift of faith in your beloved Son and in his resurrection from the dead. May that faith, more precious than gold, be for us our strength, our joy and our salvation.*

Third Sunday of Easter

In the first reading (Acts 2:14, 22-33) Peter addresses the crowd that has gathered about the disciples on the first Pentecost Sunday. He points to the resurrection of Jesus as the fulfilment of Psalm 15, which features as today's responsorial psalm.

We meet Peter again in the second reading (1 Peter 1:17-21) but this time it is through a letter of his. In it he exhorts Christian people to remember that they have been ransomed 'by the precious blood of a lamb without stain' and that through him they now have faith in God 'who raised him from the dead... so that you would have faith and hope'.

The gospel (Luke 24:13-35) suggests that belief in the resurrection of Jesus is not always easy to come by: the two disciples on the way to Emmaus found it hard to believe that Jesus had risen, even though at that moment he was there in their midst. The truth dawned upon them as they 'broke bread' in the Eucharist and then their great desire was to share the good news with others.

Psalm 15 is a psalm of confidence, and, as indicated above, the first Christians saw in it a deeper significance than its original composer could have imagined: it pointed to Jesus himself, whose body God would not 'leave... among the dead'. (This psalm seems to have been written by a priest and so the male pronoun is used throughout; but of course as the psalm stands in the liturgy it applies as much to women as to men, as much to the lay person as to the priest.)

Prayerful Ponderings

'Show us, Lord, the path of life.'

The psalm ends with the promise that the Lord will show the psalmist 'the path of life'. This sentence, which is the response to the psalm, turns that promise into a prayer; over and over again we plead: 'Show us, Lord, the path of life', and the life we have in mind is the life of the resurrection – fullness of life, eternal life.

'Preserve me, God, I take refuge in you. I say to the Lord: "You are my God. O Lord, it is you who are my portion and cup; it is you yourself who are my prize."'

Powerfully, the psalmist expresses his confidence in God; he places his trust in him, makes him his place of 'refuge', calls him not simply 'God' but 'my God' (thereby stressing the intimacy of their relationship). And he continues, describing God as his 'portion and cup'. When Israel entered the Promised Land, though the other tribes received divisions of the territory, the priestly tribe of Levi did not, because, as the Lord told them, 'I am your portion' (Numbers 18:20). The notion of 'cup' (a reference to the cup used for drawing lots) is close to that of portion: it means that God has been allotted to him – God is his life, his inheritance, his destiny. Finally, he calls God 'my prize'; centuries later Paul will use similar language, explaining that in comparison with Christ all else seems like rubbish and that his one desire is to press forward towards 'the prize' awaiting him in heaven (Philippians 3:7-16).

'I will bless the Lord who gives me counsel, who even at night directs my heart.'

He gives thanks to God, grateful for the way in which he has guided him, and is guiding him still. He is sure that even 'at night' the God who never sleeps is directing him, perhaps because he, the psalmist, often turns to him at that time, keeping vigil with him in prayer; or perhaps because he believes that in the silent hours of the night God is still at work, giving direction and purpose to his 'heart', his innermost self, and preparing him for the day that lies ahead.

'I keep the Lord ever in my sight: since he is at my right hand, I shall stand firm.'

The truth of the matter is that this devout believer has God constantly in mind, he practises the presence of God, as we might say. And it is because of the centrality of God in his life that he feels secure, he is able to 'stand firm'.

'And so my heart rejoices, my soul is glad; even my body shall rest in safety. For you will not leave my soul among the dead, nor let your beloved know decay. You will show me the path of life, the fullness of joy in your presence, at your right hand happiness for ever.'

At every level of his being – 'heart', 'body' and 'soul' – he is filled with joy because of the security that God affords him. Above all, God will not surrender him to Sheol, the place of the dead. This may not be an unambiguous expression of belief in an afterlife; nonetheless, the psalmist's confidence is such that he simply cannot imagine there ever being a time when the relationship with the Lord can be broken. As the Jerusalem Bible puts it: 'The hope, though vague as yet, is leading towards a belief in resurrection.'

Both Peter (Acts 2:22-33, see above) and Paul (Acts 13:35) quote this verse, seeing its fulfilment in the resurrection of Jesus. Now it is possible for us to pray this psalm just as it stands, and with a trust that matches the language of the song. In the Risen Jesus, the Lord has indeed shown us 'the path of life', given us the promise of 'fullness of joy' in his presence and the assurance of enjoying his company, at his 'right hand', for ever.

LET US PRAY: *Loving Father, though in your mysterious plan your Son had to die, yet you would not allow your Beloved to know decay, but raised him up to new life. Teach us to find our ultimate happiness in you alone so that one day we may share the glory of your Son's resurrection.*

Fourth Sunday of Easter

As on the other Sundays of Eastertide, the first reading today is taken from the Acts of the Apostles (2:14, 36-41), in fact from Peter's Pentecost speech, from which last Sunday's first reading was also taken. He begins with the bold announcement that, through the resurrection, 'God has made this Jesus whom you crucified both Lord [a title normally reserved for God but now given to Jesus, too] and Christ [Messiah]'; and he calls upon the people to repent and 'be baptised in the name of Jesus Christ'. We learn that three thousand responded to the invitation.

In the second reading (1 Peter 2:20-25) Peter exhorts us to find courage in times of suffering from the example of Jesus himself, who though utterly innocent suffered grievously; as his wounds have brought about our healing, so our sufferings united with his can play a part in his saving work. The innocent Lamb is also 'the shepherd and guardian of [our] souls'.

The shepherd motif appears again in the gospel (John 10:1-10) where Jesus is presented not only as the leader, the shepherd, of his sheep but also as the sheep gate which allows the sheep safe passage into the fold. The latter idea takes on added significance if we think of the shepherd lying down at night at the entrance to the sheepfold, thus providing a human gateway and protection for his sheep.

In a Liturgy of the Word where there are so many references to the theme of shepherding, it is hardly surprising that this Sunday is often known as 'Good Shepherd Sunday' and that its responsorial psalm is Psalm 22.

Prayerful Ponderings

It's only a few weeks since we considered Psalm 22 (see pp. 77-78) verse by verse. Today we can perhaps deal with it in more general terms. Then it was viewed against the backcloth of Lent and, in particular, the sufferings and death of the Lord; but now against the backcloth of his glorious resurrection.

The Risen Lord always bears the marks of the passion upon his body (his wounded hands and feet, and wounded side, will not allow us to forget that he himself has walked 'the valley of darkness' even unto death), yet today he stands before us as the Conqueror of every evil, including death, and he promises us a share in his victory. Through the Easter sacraments of baptism, confirmation and the Eucharist – in the early Church it was customary for converts to receive all three 'sacraments of initiation' at Eastertime – he has set up a personal relationship with us, pours out upon us his Holy Spirit, feeds us with his own body and blood. He will be with us – in the bad times as well as the good; like the most devoted of shepherds, he is aware of our needs and eager to meet them; his 'goodness and kindness' shadow us 'all the days of our life'. Through his rising from the dead, he has opened up the gateway to eternal life and so finally he will lead us into the glory of 'the Lord's own house' where we shall dwell 'for ever and ever'.

There is an attractive story that is often told about this most popular of psalms. In the last century two clergymen were fell-walking in the Highlands of Scotland when they came across a young shepherd boy who could neither read nor write. After chatting for a while, they recited Psalm 22 to him, and, realising that he would be unable to remember it all, they suggested that he might learn the first line by heart. As he repeated the five words – 'The Lord is my shepherd' – he could number them off on the fingers of his hand, pausing for a moment on the 'my' of the fourth finger as a way of reminding himself that the psalm was specially for him. A year later, when the two clergymen were again up in the Highlands, they called at a cottage and there to their astonishment they found a photograph of the young shepherd. The lady of the house explained that it was a picture of her son and that he had perished on the hill-side in a snow-storm that winter. 'But', she added, 'a strange thing, when he was found, he was clutching the fourth finger of his right hand.'

This beautiful psalm is mine – and yours – too.

LET US PRAY: *Lord God of peace, who brought back from the dead our Lord Jesus, the great shepherd of the sheep, make us complete in everything good so that we may do your will, working among us that which is pleasing in your sight, through Jesus Christ, to whom be glory for ever and ever (based on Hebrews 13:20).*

Fifth Sunday of Easter

The Lord has words of encouragement for his disciples in today's gospel (John 14:1-12): they are not to be troubled; he is going to prepare a place for them; he is the Way, the Truth and the Life; to have seen him is to have seen the Father; those who believe in him will perform 'even greater works' than he does himself.

The disciples must often have reflected on those words in the days beyond their Master's death and resurrection, when they were left 'alone' to face the needs of the infant Church. Today's first reading (Acts 6:1-7) shows, however, with what confidence those needs were met, even when it meant setting up a new ministry for the sake of non-Jews who were converted to the Lord; and the result? 'The word of the Lord continued to spread.'

The fact is that, as the second reading (1 Peter 2:4-9) makes clear, they saw the Lord himself as the foundation stone of the whole enterprise and themselves simply as his servants, making their contribution but above all cooperating with him.

Psalm 32 is a communal act of worship, a song of praise to God, in particular for his word and his work and his love. It is also a confident profession of trust.

Prayerful Ponderings

'May your love be upon us, O Lord, as we place all our hope in you.'

This response, which comes from the final verse of the psalm, is perhaps a liturgical addition enabling the worshippers to pray that, as all their hopes are centred upon the Lord, so their trust will be vindicated by the *hesed*, the loving faithfulness, that the Lord will show them. (It is also possible that the addition was made so that the number of lines of the psalm would match exactly the number of letters in the Hebrew alphabet.)

'Ring out your joy to the Lord, O you just; for praise is fitting for loyal hearts.'

The 'just', that is to say, the members of the congregation, are urged to praise the Lord with rejoicing. Praise, as the final words remind them (and us), is what is to be expected of those who are loyal servants of the Lord. In the prophet Isaiah (43:21) we find God describing Israel as 'the people whom I formed for myself so that they might declare my praise'. And at every Mass, in the words which introduce the Preface of the Eucharistic Prayer, we declare that: 'It is right to give him thanks and praise.'

'Give thanks to the Lord upon the harp, with a ten-stringed lute sing him songs.'

The praise and the 'thanks' are to be given not only with voice – 'sing him songs' – but also with musical instruments – 'harp' and 'ten-stringed lute' – and, we may reasonably assume, with dance as well. Dance is not expressly mentioned, but harp and lute were regularly used to accompany dancing in Israel's worship.

'For the word of the Lord is faithful and all his works to be trusted.'

We have better reason than the psalmist to praise the Lord for his 'word' and his 'works' (which summarise all his activity); we have witnessed them in the life, death and glorification of Jesus. Indeed, his words and actions are to be identified with those of the Father: 'My Father is still working', he tells those who protest at his curing on the Sabbath, 'and I am working' (John 5:17); and to his disciples he gives the assurance: 'the words that I say to you I do not speak on my own, but the Father who dwells in me does his works' (John 14:10). Jesus' words are not only 'faithful' in that they contain truth; they are also 'to be trusted' in that they work the work of God and further his purposes. It is because his words/works are 'to be trusted' that the apostles were heartened by what he told them at the Last Supper (gospel) and inspired with confidence to tackle the needs of the Church (second reading).

'The Lord loves justice and right and fills the earth with his love.'

The words and works of the Lord are not only faithful and to be trusted, they are also just and righteous; 'justice' and righteousness are often paired in this fashion to describe God's commitment to the covenant. But beyond words and works, beyond justice and righteousness – though filling them all – is God's abundant and unchanging 'love'

'The Lord looks on those who revere him, on those who hope in his love, to rescue their souls from death, to keep them alive in famine.'

The notion of God looking down on earth is one which expresses both his 'distance' from the world and at the same time his attentiveness to it. In particular, he is attentive to 'those who revere him', those who trust in his abiding 'love'. The psalmist envisages this attentiveness in terms of protection from whatever threatens life – such as sickness or famine. Because of our Risen Lord, we see God's attentiveness in terms of provision here and now of the 'bread of eternal life' and beyond death itself a life that will know no end.

LET US PRAY: *We give thanks, Lord, and we give praise because of the words and works and love of your Son, Jesus. May we follow him, the Way, confident that we can trust him, the Truth, and certain in the knowledge that he will be for us Life that is never-ending.*

Sixth Sunday of Easter

Jesus promises: 'I will not leave you orphans' (John 14:15-21). The coming of the Holy Spirit will ensure on the one hand that we are not alone and on the other that all that God accomplished in his Son will transcend the barriers of time and be available to Christ's followers in every generation; they will be loved by the Trinity and the Trinity will dwell within them.

In the first reading (Acts 8:5-8, 14-17) we hear how, as a result of persecution in Jerusalem, the disciples dispersed and Philip found himself in Samaria. This became a God-given opportunity for many Samaritans to hear and respond to the good news and then, through the imposition of the hands of the apostles, to receive the Holy Spirit.

In the second reading (1 Peter 3:15-18), probably directed especially to people newly baptised (such as those in Samaria), Peter makes it clear that opposition will inevitably come their way; they must be able to offer a reasoned defence for their position but also have an unfailing trust in their Master, Jesus, who himself suffered, 'innocent though he was'.

Psalm 65 could have been written for this Sunday. As a communal song of praise and thanksgiving for God's awesome deeds, it might have been sung by the new Samaritan Christians or the recipients of Peter's letter or, for that matter, by ourselves who are the beneficiaries of God's wonderful works this very day.

Prayerful Ponderings

'Cry out with joy to God all the earth, O sing to the glory of his name. O render him glorious praise. Say to God: "How tremendous your deeds!"'

This verse suggests that this is a psalm which should be the concern of everyone, for it is addressed to 'all the earth'; and its opening words, which serve as the refrain to the whole responsorial psalm, are a reminder, constantly repeated, that we should listen and respond to the psalmist's appeal. He wants everyone to 'cry out', 'sing', 'render... praise' and 'say' – all stereotyped ways of inviting people to worship God, to praise him because of his 'tremendous deeds'. At Eastertide it is particularly fitting that we should respond to this invitation as we celebrate the wonders of the resurrection.

'"Before you all the earth shall bow; shall sing to you, sing to your name!" Come and see the works of God, tremendous his deeds among men.'

In response to the fourfold appeal of the previous verse – cry out, sing, render praise and say – we have a threefold summary of what is expected: people are to 'bow', 'sing to you', 'sing to your name'. Once again the psalmist urges us to 'come and see' – or, as we might say, to recall – the awesome 'deeds' that God has wrought on this earth.

'He turned the sea into dry land, they passed through the river dry-shod. Let our joy then be in him; he rules for ever by his might.'
This verse makes it clear that what the psalmist has in mind is the Exodus from Egypt, together with the crossing, 'dry-shod', of the Sea of Reeds. How, he seems to say, can such mighty deeds fail to fill you with 'joy', fail to convince you that the Lord is a mighty king who rules 'for ever'? As Christians, we have a new and even more awesome story to add to the record of God's 'tremendous deeds': the death and resurrection of Jesus by which new life has been won for the whole human race, the new life which every human heart longs for.

'Come and hear, all who fear God. I will tell what he did for my soul: Blessed be God who did not reject my prayer nor withhold his love from me.'
At this point in the hymn an individual steps forward to express gratitude and wonder for their own personal sharing in the deliverance won for all the people; she or he wants everyone to 'come and hear' all that God has done. In similar fashion, though we are saved as part of a people, yet each one of us has a personal faith story to tell; and there are situations where we are happy that others should hear that story, that they should join with us in giving thanks to God for all that he has done, for hearing our prayer, for allowing 'his love' to enrich our lives.

LET US PRAY: *Heavenly Father, we gladly acknowledge all your mighty deeds, especially the resurrection of your Son, Jesus, and the salvation that he has won for us. May we live our lives in a spirit of thankfulness and joy for your great goodness.*

see page 267 for the feast of the Ascension

Seventh Sunday of Easter

Last Thursday was Ascension Day. Today's first reading (Acts 1:12-14) picks up the Christian story from immediately after Jesus' ascension: the disciples – real people with real names, including Mary herself – returned to Jerusalem and went back to the upper room, there to await in prayer the coming of the Holy Spirit.

The gospel (John 17:1-11) also takes us to the upper room but this time it's the night of the Last Supper. Jesus completes his discourse to his friends; he explains that, in revealing the Father to them, he has completed the work given him to do, and now he prays that the Father may be glorified and that he himself may be glorified as the disciples come to a yet deeper knowledge and love of the Father. Such knowledge and love will become possible through the outpouring of the Holy Spirit.

In the second reading (1 Peter 4:13-16) Peter encourages his readers/listeners to be of good heart when they are called to share 'in the sufferings of Christ' for such suffering is a sign that they will share in his glory; for already they have 'the Spirit of glory, the Spirit of God resting on [them]'.

The excerpt from Psalm 26 which we pray today breathes the air of trust and confidence that radiates from the other readings.

Prayerful Ponderings

'I am sure I shall see the Lord's goodness in the land of the living.'
This response is a bold statement of confidence in the Lord; and the other verses are a filling-out of that initial statement. Its constant repetition in the psalm may serve to remind us that the expression of trust was not a one-off affair but rather a theme which the psalmist felt the need to repeat time and again throughout life. We could hardly do better than follow that example.

'The Lord is my light and my help; whom shall I fear? The Lord is the stronghold of my life; before whom shall I shrink?'
I know more than one person who in a period of great inner turmoil found immense comfort in the gentle repetition of this verse. 'The Lord' is 'light' at those times in life when I seem to be surrounded by darkness; the Lord is 'help' when I feel unable to cope with life's demands; the Lord is a 'stronghold' when I am all too conscious of my personal weakness. And so deep down I know that I need 'fear' no other human being, need 'shrink' back in the face of no one. It is the kind of strengthening often associated with the Holy Spirit, the Comforter *par excellence*.

'There is one thing I ask of the Lord, for this I long, to live in the house of the Lord, all the days of my life, to savour the sweetness of the Lord, to behold his temple.'
The psalmist begs for the 'one thing' that every human heart yearns

for (even without always realising it) – the presence of God. For the people of the Old Testament the special place of his presence, 'the house of the Lord', was the Temple. Vatican II taught us that at Mass, his presence is manifold: in the actions of the priest, in the proclamation of the word, in the consecrated bread and wine, in the assembly itself. But ultimately the presence that we long for is the face-to-face presence in heaven. Only then shall we 'savour [his] sweetness' to the full.

'O Lord, hear my voice when I call; have mercy and answer. Of you my heart has spoken: "Seek his face."'
Despite the protestations of trust – and there is no reason to doubt their sincerity – the psalmist is well aware of dangers and difficulties, and so the earnest prayer is made that the Lord will 'hear', 'have mercy', 'answer'. There are times when we may find ourselves in much the same situation: confident of God and his concern for us, yet still feeling the need to cry out for his help. Even at such times there is another, more fundamental, plea: it comes from the very depths of 'my heart' – 'seek his face'. Ultimately, the finding of his face is all that matters.

LET US PRAY: *Lord our God, we believe that you are indeed our light, our help and our stronghold; in the dark times of life may your Holy Spirit comfort us and may our trust in you hold firm until that day when we see you, with the Son and the Spirit, in the face-to-face vision of our heavenly home.*

Pentecost

Today marks the end or, better, the climax of the Great Fifty Days of Eastertide: the coming of the Holy Spirit, and with it the birth of the Church, completes the redeeming work of Christ.

The gospel (John 20:19-23) takes us back to the beginning of the Easter season and so reminds us that the gift of the Spirit sets the seal on Jesus' death and resurrection. It is a gift which brings with it the further gifts of peace and forgiveness of sin.

The first reading (Acts 2:1-11) retells the story of what happened on the first Pentecost day. The advent of the Spirit was like a new creation, the Church was born and the estrangement of the tower of Babel reversed as the disciples, now filled with the Spirit, discovered that what they said was understood by all their hearers, though they were of different races and different languages.

In the second reading (1 Corinthians 12:3-7, 12-13) we are given a glimpse of the Church in Corinth: it has come to life, thanks to the Holy Spirit. That Spirit binds all together in a single body, is the source of a variety of spiritual gifts and, dwelling in the heart of each of the baptised, makes it possible for them to acknowledge that 'Jesus is Lord'.

The author of Psalm 103 – in today's Mass we have only a few excerpts from it – is not only a person of deep faith, one who sees that nature bears the fingerprints of its Maker and is kept in being by his Spirit, but also a poet who knows how to use language to celebrate what he sees. It reads like a poetical version of the creation account in Genesis 1.

Prayerful Ponderings

'**Bless the Lord, my soul! Lord God, how great you are! How many are your works, O Lord! The earth is full of your riches.**'
As you hear these words, you can almost imagine the poet standing beside the Creator as he gazes upon his work of creation and sees that it is good, very good. The psalmist gasps with wonder and delight: 'Lord God, how great you are!' The whole world seems to be alive with his masterpieces. He bids his 'soul' to 'bless the Lord', as though he wants his innermost self to be involved in the wonder and the worship. On this day we are invited to share the psalmist's praise, remembering however that the Holy Spirit has worked a new and even more wonderful creation, through which we are enabled to call upon God as Abba (dear Father).

'**You take back your spirit, they die, returning to the dust from which they came. You send forth your spirit, they are created; and you renew the face of the earth.**'
After reflecting on the countless creatures God has made, the psalmist marvels at the way he has provided for them all: their very 'spirit' (the Hebrew word also means 'breath') comes as gift from God; should he take it away, 'they die'; should he restore it again, 'they are created' and the whole of creation is renewed.

A slightly amended form of this verse, making it into a prayer that God will 'send forth [his] Spirit [spelt with a capital "S"] and renew the face of the earth', is the refrain for today's responsorial psalm; we are surely meant to realise that if we give thanks to God for the gift of our life's breath, still more must we thank him that, through the gift of the Holy Spirit, he shares his own life with us: we are indeed renewed and transformed.

'May the glory of the Lord last for ever! May the Lord rejoice in his works!'
These words come towards the end of the psalm. It is as though the psalmist is almost lost for words and can only say that he wants the Lord's 'glory' to go on and on for ever and at the same time wants the Lord to go on rejoicing in all 'his works'.

'May my thoughts be pleasing to him. I find my joy in the Lord.'
Finally, the plea that the psalmist's own 'thoughts', the psalmist's meditation, all that has been said in this psalm, may be like a 'pleasing' offering to the Lord. It is 'in the Lord' that the psalmist, and we too, find our best and lasting 'joy.'

LET US PRAY: *Creator God, you make all things new; come and, on this day of Pentecost, breathe your Holy Spirit into us anew so that we may work with you for the renewal of the whole world.*

The Most Holy Trinity

Every Sunday is a celebration of the Blessed Trinity, but each year this Sunday, the one following the end of Eastertide, is set aside in honour of the central mystery of our faith.

We could not expect to find a direct reference to the Trinity in the Old Testament, but today's first reading, taken from the book of Exodus (34:4-6, 8-9), is an inspired choice. It describes how, shortly after the people had sinned by worshipping a golden calf, Moses returned to Mount Sinai to intercede for them, and there received the revelation of God's mercy, compassion and readiness to forgive. If God's attitude towards his creatures is one of love and tenderness, does not that at least hint that there might be relationships of love and tenderness within God himself?

In fact the gospel (John 3:16-18) for today not only speaks once again of God's 'external' love, his love for the world of his creatures, but also reveals that he has a Son, the fruit of 'internal' love within the Godhead.

The second reading, taken from 2 Corinthians (13:11-13), is still clearer: it uses a formula, well known in the early Church, which indicates that the first Christians believed that God (Father), Jesus Christ (Son) and the Holy Spirit are threefold and yet one, a common source of blessing – three Persons, one God, as later theology will express it.

Today's responsorial psalm comes not from the Psalter, but from the book of the prophet Daniel (3:52-56).

Prayerful Ponderings

Just as today's psalm comes from an unexpected quarter, so these reflections will take a somewhat unexpected form: they will offer an overall view rather than a detailed discussion of each verse.

To begin with, today's responsorial psalm reminds us that it is not only within the Psalter that psalms are to be found: they also appear in other places in the Old Testament (and in the New), though in such cases they are usually referred to as canticles (little songs). One of the ways in which canticles differ from the psalms proper (if we may call them that) is that they are found in their historical context, so that it is usually possible to say who originally said/sang them and also the situation in which it took place – a possibility scarcely ever present in the psalms.

The book of Daniel was written in about the year 165 BC. The passage in which our responsorial psalm appears tells how the Babylonian king had set up a huge golden statue which all must worship, how three young men of Israel refused to do so, how they were delated to the authorities and then thrown into a fiery furnace, and how in this dire situation they raised their voices to sing songs of praise to God. It is from the second of their songs, which is in the form of a litany, that today's psalm comes.

God's 'glorious holy name', which stands for all that he is, is to be 'blest'. He is to be blest 'in the temple of [his] glory', heaven itself, and 'on the throne of [his] kingdom', from which he reigns over all.

From that highpoint he is able to 'gaze into the depths' of his creation, and for that too he is to be blest.

The refrain is: 'To you glory and praise for evermore.' No matter what our personal difficulties and problems may be, it is scarcely likely that we shall find ourselves in such adversity as those three young men! So let us join them in their extraordinary litany, let us bless and glorify and give praise to God, but as we do so let us also be truly grateful that in faith we are able to acknowledge that God is Father full of loving tenderness, Son making us co-heirs of his glory, and Holy Spirit dwelling in our hearts – one God, Most Holy Trinity.

LET US PRAY: *Father, encompass me; Son, encircle me; Holy Spirit, enfold me; that I may live worthily of you, Most Holy Trinity, who made me and for whom I was made.*

see page 273 for the feast of the Body and Blood of Christ.

ORDINARY TIME

*Let
my prayer
rise
like incense
before
you*

ORDINARY TIME

'Apart from the seasons of Easter, Lent,
Christmas and Advent,
which have their own characteristics,
there are thirty-three or thirty-four weeks
in the course of the year which
celebrate no particular aspect of the mystery of Christ...
This period is known as ordinary time'
(General Norms for the Liturgical Year §43)

Second Sunday in Ordinary Time

'Ordinary' time – it began last week after the feast of the Baptism of our Lord – is that part of the Church's year which falls outside Advent/Christmas and Lent/Easter and so celebrates the whole mystery of Christ rather than a particular aspect of it.

In today's Mass the reading from Isaiah (49:3, 5-6) speaks of a mysterious servant of the Lord. Christians have long identified him with Jesus, who was 'formed [by God] in the womb' and sent into this world as 'the light of the nations', bringing 'salvation… to the ends of the earth'.

We are among those who through baptism have in principle received the salvation Jesus brought but that also includes, as the second reading (1 Corinthians 1:1-3) makes clear, a calling to be holy, a calling to 'take [our] place among all the saints everywhere who pray to our Lord Jesus Christ'.

In the gospel (John 1:29-34) it is John the Baptist who recognises in Jesus 'the lamb of God who takes away the sin of the world'.

Psalm 39 is the prayer of an individual who has been extricated from dreadful difficulty, which he describes – though the words do not appear in the extract of the psalm we hear today – as a 'deadly pit', and now comes to the Temple to give thanks. It's a psalm which voices the frame of mind of our Saviour who, from the moment he came into this world, delighted to do his Father's will and so was able to offer the perfect sacrifice of thanks and praise.

Prayerful Ponderings

'I waited, I waited for the Lord and he stooped down to me; he heard my cry.'
At the heart of all prayer is waiting upon God, simply being there in his presence. But the wonderful news is, as Isaiah the prophet says, that God is waiting for us, too: 'The Lord waits to be gracious to you... blessed are all those who wait for him' (30:18). It's an experience that the psalmist has known: prayer was heard and God 'stooped down to me' and rescued me from the 'pit'.

'He put a new song into my mouth, praise of our God.'
'A life of faith', wrote Henri Nouwen, 'is a life of gratitude.' Most of us tend to be more adept at asking than thanking; request comes to our lips rather more readily than does the 'new song' of thanksgiving. The psalmist is in no doubt that even gratitude is not of his own making but comes as gift from God. It's a gift for which we ought to pray.

'In the scroll of the book it stands written that I should do your will.'
The 'scroll of the book' probably refers to the Scriptures which are the revelation of God's will. The psalmist recognises this and is going to make them the compass by which his life will be directed. There is no more practical way of showing our gratitude to God than by readiness to do his will.

'You do not ask for sacrifice and offerings, but an open ear. You do not ask for holocaust and victim. Instead, here am I. My God, I delight in your law in the depth of my heart.'

In biblical times it was usual to express thanks to God by offering a bloody animal sacrifice, but the psalmist sees a nobler way – the sacrifice of mind and heart to the will of God. It was our Lord's total dedication to his Father's will that ultimately led him to Calvary and to the sacrifice which is the most perfect act of worship the world has ever seen. In the letter to the Hebrews, Jesus is depicted as reciting the words of this verse as he comes into the world. It goes on to declare that he has abolished the old-style sacrifices to replace them with his own: the sacrifice which he once offered, with the shedding of his life's blood, on Calvary and which is re-presented for us in a bloodless manner at every Mass.

'Your justice I have proclaimed in the great assembly. My lips I have not sealed; you know it, O Lord.'

'The great assembly' suggests a festival time when great crowds converged on the Temple. There the psalmist boldly bore testimony to the goodness of God, proclaimed it publicly. And we too need the Sunday gathering at Mass to proclaim our gratitude, in company with our brothers and sisters: it is our Eucharist, our great act of thanks.

'Here I am, Lord! I come to do your will.'

These words which serve as the response to the psalm are also its high point. As already mentioned, we are to think of them first of all as on the lips of Jesus; however, our earnest prayer must surely be that in some measure at least we may make them our own.

LET US PRAY: *We rejoice, Lord, in the realisation that as we wait upon you, you are always waiting for us, waiting to stoop down to us in all our needs. Keep us sensitive to the goodness you show us, make us joyful participants in the thanksgiving of the Mass and help us always to make your will the compass of our lives.*

Third Sunday in Ordinary Time

There is an obvious link between today's responsorial psalm and both the first reading and the gospel.

In the gospel Matthew (4:12-23) records how Jesus settled in Capernaum, beside the Lake of Galilee, and the evangelist sees it as the fulfilment of the prophecy mentioned in the first reading (Isaiah 8:23-9:3). When the people of Galilee, who belonged to the tribes of Zebulun and Naphtali, were being deported to Assyria in the sixth century before the birth of Christ, the prophet Isaiah had promised that their land, then in deep shadow, would one day witness a great light in its midst. Jesus is that light: 'I am the light of the world. Anyone who follows me will not be walking in the dark' (John 8:12).

But if we are to walk in his light we must take care to avoid all that leads to division and disharmony among God's people. In the second reading (1 Corinthians 1:10-13, 17), Paul rounds upon Christians who have split into factions in the name of the particular evangeliser who had brought them the gospel. He fiercely proclaims that it is in the one Jesus that all have been baptised, and it is that same Jesus who was crucified for all. He alone – not any of his ministers – is our light; we must be one in him.

Psalm 26, originally addressed to Yahweh, the God of Israel, is an eloquent prayer of trust, though unfortunately we have only a brief excerpt from the psalm in today's Mass. From the time of his resurrection Jesus' disciples, under the guidance of the Holy Spirit, came to recognise that he too is to be addressed as 'Lord', and so Psalm 26 can now be addressed directly to him.

Prayerful Ponderings

'The Lord is my light and my help; whom shall I fear?'
A friend of mine suffered for many years from deep depression. In her darkest and loneliest times, she told me, the only prayer that still made sense to her was this line of the psalm (which also serves as the response in today's Mass). She could cling to the assurance that, despite everything, the Lord was light (in the dark) and help (in the loneliness), and that with him on her side she need fear no one – and nothing. The Hebrew word for 'help' (*y'shu'a*) might better be translated 'salvation'; it is the word from which the name Jesus was derived: 'you are to name him Jesus, for he will save his people from their sins' (Matthew 1:21).

'The Lord is the stronghold of my life; before whom shall I shrink?'
Another bold declaration of confidence: if the forces of evil should seem to threaten my very existence, even then I would not shrink back in fear, for in fact the Lord is my 'stronghold', God's own strength is on my side. A similar assertion is made by Paul (Romans 8:31): 'If God is for us, who can be against us?'

'There is one thing I ask of the Lord, for this I long, to live in the house of the Lord, all the days of my life...'
Like Martha's sister Mary, who sought 'the one thing needed' (Luke 10:38-42), the psalmist has only one request to make, that he may

'live in the house of the Lord all the days of my life'. The words need not be taken literally as a desire to become one of the priests or Levites who dwell permanently in the Temple, but rather can be seen as the desire to experience what their way of life typified – life in the abiding presence of God. And that is possible anywhere, even in the midst of a busy life, for, as St Teresa of Avila taught us, our God walks among the pots and pans.

'...to savour the sweetness of the Lord, to behold his temple.'
An important consequence of 'living in the presence of God' is growing awareness of 'the sweetness' or, as we might say, the beauty and attractiveness of the Lord. The psalmist may in fact have wanted to 'behold' the Lord's 'temple' in Jerusalem, a vivid symbol of the wonder and splendour of God's presence in the midst of his people. For us Christians, there is the privilege of beholding, in the sense of recognising, God's living presence not only in church but also within ourselves: 'Know you not that you are the (living) temple of God?' (1 Corinthians 3:16).

'I am sure I shall see the Lord's goodness in the land of the living.'
Possibly this sentence should read: 'Unless I were sure I would see the Lord's goodness...', the implication being that without such awareness I would not be praying this prayer at all. It's an idea which we can readily warm to: in the last resort prayer is an act of faith, and for the Christian it's a faith which looks forward to the face-to-face vision of God's goodness in heaven, 'the land' of everlasting life.

'Hope in him, hold firm and take heart. Hope in the Lord!'
The psalmist has a final word of encouragement for whoever will listen, an exhortation not to lose heart but to stand firm and wait upon the Lord. He is always worth waiting for.

LET US PRAY: *Lord Jesus, you are our light, our stronghold and our salvation. Like Peter and Andrew, James and John, may we follow you trustingly, knowing that you enlighten us in times of darkness, strengthen us in moments of weakness, and lead us to salvation in the vision of the goodness of God in the land of the living.*

Fourth Sunday
in Ordinary Time

Psalm 145 is the first of a group of psalms sometimes referred to as the Final Hallel, the last of several similar groups in which each psalm begins and ends with 'Alleluia' (Praise the Lord). ('Alleluia', as you will notice, is an alternative response to today's responsorial psalm.) It's a psalm which contrasts the fickleness of human beings with the absolute faithfulness of God. It invites us to praise him because he is on the side of the poor and the lowly, and is determined that they shall receive justice.

It's a psalm which resonates with all three readings of today's Mass. With the first, because Zephaniah (2:3; 3:12-13), who is usually so gloomy in his prophecies, promises here that the Lord will raise up a 'humble and lowly people' who will 'seek refuge in the name of the Lord'. With the second, because Paul (1 Corinthians 1:26-31) declares that those who became Christians in the great metropolis of Corinth were not the wise, influential and noble, but those who were 'foolish and weak by human reckoning', indeed 'those who are nothing at all'.

And finally with the gospel (Matthew 5:1-12) because there Jesus speaks of the beatitude, the happiness, of those who are lowly of heart but seek the Lord.

Prayerful Ponderings

'How happy are the poor in spirit; theirs is the kingdom of heaven.'
This is the first of the 'Beatitudes'. Each of them indicates an attitude of mind and heart which leads to beatitude, true happiness. To avoid a purely 'economic' interpretation of this beatitude, Jesus speaks of the 'poor in spirit', that is to say, those who in spirit, in the depths of their being, recognise their total need of God, put their complete trust in him, await everything from his hands. Often it is those who have least of this world's goods who are most open to God. Such people, says Jesus, already have the future kingdom in their possession.

'It is the Lord who keeps faith for ever, who is just to those who are oppressed.'
As pointed out above, this is a psalm which, without belittling human efforts, insists that the Lord, in comparison with all ephemeral helpers, is eternally trustworthy. Other benefactors may, in good faith, make generous promises but there is no guarantee that they will live to keep them. That cannot happen with the Lord; and his eyes – and heart – are especially directed towards those who are oppressed in any way.

'It is he who gives bread to the hungry, the Lord, who sets prisoners free. It is the Lord who give sight to the blind, who raises up those who are bowed down...'
In the synagogue at Nazareth Jesus read a passage from Isaiah 61:

'The Spirit of the Lord is upon me... he has appointed me to bring good news to the poor... to proclaim release to captives and recovery of sight to the blind, to let the oppressed go free'; and then he added: 'Today this scripture has been fulfilled in your hearing' (Luke 4:16-21). He might just as easily have used the words of this psalm as a way of summarising the programme of his mission. His miracles – feeding the hungry, giving sight to the blind, freeing people from their infirmities – are all indications of his personal option for the 'poor'.

'...the Lord, who protects the stranger and upholds the widow and orphan.'
From its own history, as interpreted by the prophets, Israel learned of God's compassion for the helpless and marginalised. In fact, its laws specifically sought to protect the vulnerable members of society, such as 'strangers', who depend upon the good will of the host nation, and 'widows and orphans', who are socially disadvantaged. Thus: 'You will not... oppress aliens... You will not ill-treat widows or orphans' (Exodus 22:21-23).

'It is the Lord who loves the just but thwarts the path of the wicked.'
Running through this psalm is the implication that those who know how God treats the poor will strive to follow his example. Those who do so are the 'just' and they are recipients of his love; but the 'wicked' have no concern for the poor; they cut themselves off from the effects of God's love, and their scheming, which so often is blind to the needs of the poor, will not finally prosper.

'The Lord will reign for ever, Zion's God, from age to age.'
Jesus in his very person is God's 'good news to the poor'. Today he
has no means of continuing his mission except through us. Work
for justice is an integral part of the Church's mission. It is in the
measure that we fulfil our responsibilities in this regard that 'the
Lord will reign' in our world.

LET US PRAY: *Lord Jesus, you praise those who 'hunger and thirst for
justice'. Teach us to be aware of our obligations and to fulfil them so that
we may be true sons and daughters of our compassionate Father, who reigns
with you and the Holy Spirit.*

Fifth Sunday
in Ordinary Time

Psalm 111, which we pray in today's Mass, and Psalm 110 are a pair in that both begin with the call to praise, 'Alleluia', both are similar in style and structure, and both are alphabetical (each line of the two psalms begins with successive letters of the Hebrew alphabet, though of course this does not show up in translation). However, whereas the latter is concerned with God, the former is concerned with the truly upright person. Nonetheless, the two descriptions have much in common. A good person, the psalmist seems to say, is by that very fact a God-like person; to praise such an individual is indeed an 'Alleluia', praise of God.

In one way or another, today's readings take up the same idea: the first (Isaiah 58:7-10) focuses on the need to act, like the Lord, with justice, to help the needy and to behave with integrity, while in the gospel (Matthew 5:13-16) Jesus tells his disciples that they are to be 'salt of the earth' and 'light of the world', living their lives in such a way that their light will shine in the sight of all, so that 'seeing your good works, they may give the praise to your Father in heaven'.

And the second reading (1 Corinthians 2:1-5) shows how Paul behaved in a Christ-like way: he did not try to win over the Corinthians with 'any show of oratory or philosophy' but with words about 'the crucified Christ', with a humble demeanour and with 'the power of the Spirit'.

Prayerful Ponderings

'The good man is a light in the darkness for the upright.'
This response sums up the psalm. The 'good man' is the person, man or woman, who delights in the Lord's commandments. Such people are blessed by God and their goodness overflows like a blessing upon others; their example is an encouragement to all who are trying to live upright lives. Their impact is compared to that of a light in darkness. In the psalmist's day, the 'darkness' of the night meant total blackness, unrelieved by any kind of artificial lighting, and so even the smallest light was welcome — and so comforting!

'He is a light in the darkness for the upright: he is generous, merciful and just.'
The portrait of the good person continues through succeeding verses. All the dealings of such an individual are characterised by generosity, mercy and justice — the very traits which are attributed to God himself in Psalm 110. Again a reminder that the followers of the Lord are meant to reveal something of the goodness of the Lord to others.

'The good man takes pity and lends, he conducts his affairs with honour.'
The attributes of the good person, which have just been alluded to, take practical shape in a willingness to lend freely to those who are in need and absolute fairness in all his or her dealings. As one

modern translation puts it, such a person 'runs his business honestly'; whatever our position in life, our behaviour is to be marked by integrity.

'The just man will never waver: he will be remembered for ever.'
A significant feature of the righteous is their dependability and trustworthiness. Indeed the psalmist goes so far as to say of such people what was said of God in the previous psalm, that they create an undying memorial. We see this of course in the saints but even among those who will never be canonised there are many whose goodness of life will be remembered long after they are dead. Mary McAleese, President of Ireland, provides a wonderful example in her book *Reconciled Being*, where she talks about her aged grandmother whose life bore clearly the imprint of the many hours she spent in prayer, in terms of the love and gentleness she showed towards others.

'He has no fear of evil news; with a firm heart he trusts in the Lord. With a steadfast heart he will not fear.'
The just are no more isolated from evil than are the wicked; but their strength lies in their complete trust in the Lord. Despite their own natural weakness, they have hearts that are steadfast and fear-free. It was perhaps such a person who composed the comforting saying: 'I do not know what the future holds in store, but I do know who holds the future in His hands.'

'Open-handed, he gives to the poor; his justice stands firm for ever. His head will be raised in glory.'
Once again the point is made that the God-like person is generous

to the poor. With even greater confidence than the psalmist, we can say that the good deeds of such a person have everlasting consequences; they will lead to a head 'raised in [eternal] glory'.

LET US PRAY: *You have made it clear, Lord, that those who claim to be your followers must make good their claim by the way they live their lives. In your goodness, help us to become salt to the earth and light to the world for the praise and glory of your holy name.*

Sixth Sunday
in Ordinary Time

Today's first reading (Ecclesiasticus 15:15-20) teaches us that though God's law is for our good, yet, as a supreme sign of his love, he has given us the gift of free will. That means that we must take responsibility for our actions; even if we choose to disobey, God is still in control of the universe.

Jesus, in the gospel (Matthew 5:17-37), announces that he has come not 'to abolish the Law or the Prophets... but to complete them', to reveal their hidden depths.

Today's responsorial psalm, Psalm 118, is the bumper psalm in the whole of the Psalter. Its one hundred and seventy-six verses, all devoted to the Law, are divided into twenty-two sections, one for each of the twenty-two letters of the Hebrew alphabet. It's as though the psalmist were saying: 'Look, here's the A to Z of God's Law, and all you need to know about it.' It may even have been composed in this fashion to make it (somewhat!) easier to memorise.

However, for the people of Israel, the word 'Law' (*Torah*) did not have the narrow legalistic connotations that it has for us. In fact the first five books of the Bible were known as the Torah, because they reveal the story of God's loving plans for his people and what he expects of them. So 'Torah' means instruction, something that shows us the way, reveals God's will; not so much a code of rules to be observed as a way of life to be followed. In the brief responsorial psalm we are given just a sample of what this long psalm has to offer.

Prayerful Ponderings

'They are happy whose life is blameless, who follow God's law!'
This extraordinary psalm begins with a beatitude. It might be translated: 'O the happiness, the blessedness, of the person who lives a blameless life, blameless because lived in accordance with God's will.' The revelation of his will is something in which to delight, something for which to be grateful, indeed, something to be loved; as the psalmist expresses it later in this psalm: 'My soul obeys your will and loves it dearly.'

'They are happy those who do his will, seeking him with all their hearts.'
This is clearly a restatement of what was said in the opening verse: those who are committed to doing God's will enjoy a unique happiness. But this time the idea is given a richer meaning by the addition of the words 'seeking him with all their hearts'. Doing God's will is not simply a matter of obeying orders – though obviously the keeping of his commandments is part of it – but rather a whole-hearted seeking of God himself.

'You have laid down your precepts to be obeyed with care. May my footsteps be firm to obey your statutes.'
In this long psalm, the poet makes use of various synonyms for law; here we meet two of them – 'precepts' and 'statutes'. Rather than

teasing out subtle differences of meaning between the different words, it is perhaps enough to see their usage as a poetic device which enables the poet to ring the changes and so bring variety into his work. The final words of this verse underline the fact that the Law, far from being some abstract notion, actually directs us into the way we should walk. How right, therefore, that we should beg that our 'footsteps' may be held 'firm' in that way.

'Bless your servant and I shall live and obey your word.'
The whole of Psalm 118 is, as we have noted, a lengthy meditation on the Law, but from time to time specific requests are made. Here is one, in which the psalmist asks that God may bless him by enabling him to 'live', that is, live a life worthy of the name, and that means a life of obedience to God's word ('word' being yet another synonym for law).

'Open my eyes that I may consider the wonders of your law.'
Here is another request. This time it is for clearness of vision. Just as the 'scales' had to be removed from Paul's eyes (Acts 9:18) before he could learn the truth about Jesus, so, in company with the psalmist, we plead to be set free from any blindness that would stand in the way of our recognising the wonderful nature of the divine instruction.

'Teach me the demands of your statutes and I will keep them to the end. Train me to observe your law, to keep it with my heart.'
The requests continue, and they bring this section of the psalm to a fitting end. Since God's will is all-important, the psalmist prays –

it must surely be our prayer too – first to understand clearly what the Lord wants of him and secondly for the grace to respond with willing and generous heart.

LET US PRAY: *Lord God, help us to discern your will for us and to follow it not grudgingly but with an unselfish, loving heart, knowing always that in your will is our peace.*

Seventh Sunday in Ordinary Time

'Be holy, for I, the Lord your God, am holy' (Leviticus 19:1-2, 17-18) is a key expression in the liturgical handbook Leviticus, reminding us that the ultimate purpose of law-keeping is to be like our God; sometimes it appears in abbreviated form, 'I am the Lord', as in today's reading. It also serves as a link between all the readings, including the responsorial psalm.

Jesus taught that the Temple in Jerusalem was a symbol of himself: once risen from the dead, he would be the new temple of God, the special place of the divine presence. Paul goes further (1 Corinthians 3:16-23): if the body of the risen Christ is the temple of God, then the whole Christian community makes up with him one spiritual temple. As such we are called to live in accordance with our dignity, to be holy as the Lord Jesus is holy.

The same truth is highlighted in the gospel (Matthew 5:38-48), which is our Lord's commentary on the passage from Leviticus, a commentary summed up in the injunction: 'You must therefore be perfect just as your heavenly Father is perfect.' Thus, though the *lex talionis,* 'eye for eye and tooth for tooth', was aimed at keeping acts of revenge within limits, Jesus sets different standards – turn the other cheek, surrender your cloak, walk the extra mile, don't turn away from the borrower. Similarly, the command to 'love your neighbour as yourself' was never meant to imply that you might hate your enemy, though apparently that was the way it was often read by many of Jesus' contemporaries; on the contrary, to be like the heavenly Father means to love your enemies, to pray for your persecutors.

And the psalm, a splendid prayer of gratitude to God for his mercy, presents him as filled with compassion and love (Psalm 102).

Prayerful Ponderings

'My soul, give thanks to the Lord, all my being, bless his holy name. My soul, give thanks to the Lord and never forget all his blessings.'

In the Psalter it is customary for hymns, that is, psalms in praise of the Almighty, to begin with an invitation to give praise and/or thanks to God. Somewhat unusually, in this psalm the invitation, twice repeated, is directed to the psalmist himself; it is an attempt to arouse the psalmist, and all worshippers who use these words, to recognise, 'never forget', and to acknowledge with 'all [their] being', from the depths of their hearts, all that God has done for them.

'It is he who forgives all your guilt, who heals every one of your ills, who redeems your life from the grave, who crowns you with love and compassion.'

The reasons for 'blessing' God become clear in this and the following verses – they are because he:

- 'forgives all your guilt'
- 'heals every one of your ills'
- 'redeems your life from the grave'
- 'crowns you with love and compassion'.

All these motives for grateful praise are woven into Henry Lyte's well-loved hymn, 'Praise, my soul, the King of heaven': 'Ransomed, healed, restored, forgiven, who like me his praise should sing?'

'The Lord is compassion and love, slow to anger and rich in mercy. He does not treat us according to our sins nor repay us according to our faults.'

This verse repeats almost word for word one of Israel's oldest and most important theological statements, a statement which might be described as the creed of the people of God. It is to be found originally in Exodus 34:6-7 where, while Moses hides in a cleft in the rock, God passes by and in doing so leaves his own self-portrait. His characteristics are 'compassion' or, better, graciousness and 'love', that steadfast love which is the supreme element of his goodness, making him utterly reliable in every situation and responsible for 'all… blessings' (see first verse). He is 'slow to anger' and so, in marked contrast with us, quicker to forgive than to be angry, and he is 'rich in mercy' – in Hebrew 'mercy' is associated with the word for 'womb' and so suggests the mother-like quality of God's love. Even if a woman were to forget the child of her womb, the Lord promises through Isaiah, 'yet I will never forget you' (Isaiah 49:15); that is why we are not treated as 'our sins' and 'faults' deserve.

'As far as the east is from the west so far does he remove our sins. As a father has compassion on his sons, the Lord has pity on those who fear him.'

To show how utterly God rids us of our sins, the psalmist resorts to two analogies: first, God is like a champion thrower who is able to hurl our sins 'as far as the east is from the west' – from here to

Australia, as we might say! Secondly, he has not only mother-love (see previous verse) but father-love, too; he understands his children better than any parent could, and again we are reminded that God's compassion is a caring and a concern for us which overrides the anger we might expect.

LET US PRAY: *Lord, we are overwhelmed at the extent of your compassionate love, and since your holiness expresses itself supremely in that way, may we, who are called to be perfect as our heavenly Father is perfect, strive to be compassionate and loving towards our neighbour.*

Eighth Sunday
in Ordinary Time

The response to the psalm – 'In God alone is my soul at rest' – provides a useful point of entry into today's readings. The first of them (Isaiah 49:14-15) gives the reason for such complete trust: God's love for us is keener and stronger than the most intimate of human bonds, so that even if a mother should forget her child, the Lord will never forget us.

While Isaiah speaks of our Mother-God, the gospel (Matthew 6:24-34) refers to our Father-God, but the message is the same: there is no room for worry and distress if we place all things in God's hands. Should we doubt it, we need only look at the way God cares for the flowers of the field and the birds of the air – and we are worth so much more than any of them!

Of course trust in God does not relieve us of responsibility: we must make prudent provision for the future and, as Paul shows in the second reading (1 Corinthians 4:1-5), we are all stewards 'entrusted with the mysteries of God' – called to cooperate with the Lord for the sake of the kingdom – and as such must prove ourselves to be 'worthy of his trust'.

Psalm 61 is one of a small category known as 'psalms of Confidence', which are amongst the most attractive compositions in the Psalter. For the most part they have a simple format: they begin with an affirmation of trust in God and then, throughout the rest of the psalm, unfold the significance of that trust.

Prayerful Ponderings

'In God alone is my soul at rest; my help comes from him.'
Here is the opening declaration of trust in God; it, or at any rate the first part of it, is the refrain of today's responsorial psalm. Literally, it speaks of waiting in silence, but, as the following verses show, the sense is not of remaining speechless but rather of being still and at peace within. It is a stillness which arises from the fact that from God comes 'my help', or better 'my salvation' (as in NRSV). The Hebrew word which, in this and the succeeding lines, is translated 'alone' might more accurately be rendered 'truly'; it's almost as though the psalmist were saying: 'Believe it or not but…' and so it adds emphasis to the assertion that follows.

'He alone is my rock, my stronghold, my fortress: I stand firm.'
A series of images – 'rock', 'stronghold', 'fortress' – sums up what God means to the psalmist. They are the traditional ways in which Israel spoke of God, the outcome of what they had discovered about him throughout their history. The psalmist, who, like ourselves, belongs to and is sustained by a community of faith, expresses his own personal belief; and boldly adds that in that belief 'I stand firm'.

'In God alone be at rest, my soul; for my hope comes from him. He alone is my rock, my stronghold, my fortress: I stand firm.'
The psalm began with a statement about finding rest and stillness

in God who is the source of our trust; it is now repeated but in the form of a plea or self-exhortation that the psalmist's 'soul', or innermost being, may find such stillness and 'rest'. And again there is the confident affirmation that God, and 'he alone', is able to provide the rock-like security on which such trust can be founded. 'I stand firm' might equally well be translated 'I shall not be moved'.

In the earlier verse God is said to bring 'help' or salvation (which seems to look to what has happened in the past), while in this verse he brings 'hope' (which looks more precisely to the future).

'In God is my safety and glory, the rock of my strength.'
The reasons for trust are piled up one upon another. God spells 'safety', general well-being; 'glory', literally, heaviness, and so reliability; and rock-like 'strength'. What more could we ask for? (If our Jewish forebears in the faith had such trust in God, how much firmer should be the hope of those who know of the incarnation, death and resurrection of his only Son!)

'Take refuge in God, all you people. Trust him at all times. Pour out your hearts before him.'
Turning to the assembly, the psalmist calls upon the 'people' to learn from the experience that he has shared with them, so that they too will come to place their 'trust' in the Lord in all circumstances and have courage to 'pour out [their] hearts before him', by confiding to him their deepest feelings, including their complaints – and even their disappointments with him.

LET US PRAY: *O Lord, you reveal yourself to us as one who has the strength, dependability and gentleness of both a father and a mother; we thank you for that revelation and we follow the example of the psalmist in declaring our complete trust in you.*

Ninth Sunday
in Ordinary Time

The book of Deuteronomy takes the form of a series of discourses, delivered by Moses just before his death. In today's first reading (11:18, 26-28, 32) he declares that fidelity to God's word is a matter of blessing or curse, of life or death. Following Moses' advice literally, Jews bind a text of the Law in a small container around their forehead and hand when they engage in worship. In doing so they are declaring in action that God and his word are the steadfast rock of their lives.

A similar message is found in the gospel (Matthew 7:21-27): Jesus ends the Sermon on the Mount by announcing that whoever listens to his word and acts upon it is like a wise person who builds on a rock, while those who ignore his word are like the fool who builds upon sand.

In its own way, the refrain of the responsorial psalm takes up the same theme: the psalmist looks to the Lord as rock and refuge. Taken as a whole, Psalm 30 is a cry for help in time of distress – indeed, one verse from the psalm (though it does not appear in today's excerpt) was prayed by Jesus as he was dying on the cross – it leaves us in no doubt that the psalmist knew what it means to waver; only in God can one find courage and reason for hope.

In the second reading (Romans 3:21-25, 28) Paul, like the psalmist, acknowledges that our hope and justification come as 'free gift' from God through the redeeming work of Christ. It is God, and he alone, who is our rock.

Prayerful Ponderings

'In you, O Lord, I take refuge. Let me never be put to shame. In your justice, set me free, hear me and speedily rescue me.'
The psalmist, who is no stranger to problems and uncertainties, expresses a confidence that cannot be explained except by complete trust in the Lord. Only the Lord can provide safe 'refuge' from every enemy and so save us from being 'put to shame'. Everything depends upon his willingness to help, 'his righteousness', rather than upon anything we might do. The psalmist does not hesitate to urge God to hurry to the rescue: 'hear me and speedily rescue me' – the kind of prayer that we often feel tempted to utter!

'Be a rock of refuge for me, a mighty stronghold to save me, for you are my rock, my stronghold. For your name's sake, lead me and guide me.'
'Rock of refuge', 'mighty stronghold' – these are typical images, twice repeated, to depict the steadfastness of God, though possibly there is an indication here that the psalmist has sought 'refuge', in the sense of sanctuary from his enemies, in some holy place. In any event, by speaking of God in this way, the psalmist already feels reassured and is ready to beg that God will offer the leadership and the guidance that are needed, not simply for the sake of the one who prays but 'for your name's sake'.

'Let your face shine on your servant. Save me in your love.'
God's 'face' is pictured as shining; it is lit up by a smile, the comforting smile that brings consolation to 'your servant', so that now the prayer is simply that salvation from present troubles may come from 'your love', that affection which arises from God's covenant bond with his people. It's a frame of mind that is reflected in 2 Timothy: 'I know in whom I have put my trust, and I have no doubt at all that he is able to safeguard until that Day what I have entrusted to him' (1:12).

'Be strong, let your heart take courage, all who hope in the Lord.'
In the light of personal experience, the psalmist feels impelled to invite others, including those who use this psalm, to follow his example. So long as they are prepared to put their trust 'in the Lord', their hearts can 'take courage', whatever befalls them.

LET US PRAY: *In the dark days of life, Lord, we, like your Son Jesus, need someone upon whom we can depend without fear of being let down; may we find that someone, our rock of assurance, in you, our dear heavenly Father.*

Tenth Sunday
in Ordinary Time

Hosea's personal experience of an unfaithful wife made him deeply aware of the steadfastness of God's love for his people. In the first reading (6:3-6), he draws a comparison between God's love for Israel, which is as sure as the coming of the dawn, and Israel's love of God, which is as fleeting as morning dew. Any attempt to cover up unfaithfulness by means of sacrifices is of no avail, for what God wants is love, covenant faithfulness, not empty shows of devotion.

In the gospel (Matthew 9:9-13) Jesus is attacked by the Pharisees for sitting at table with 'tax collectors and sinners'; in his response, he urges them to 'learn the meaning of the words [of Hosea]: What I want is mercy [love], not sacrifice.'

The second reading (Romans 4:18-25) also reflects the emphasis that runs through the other readings; it shows that Abraham found salvation not through mere observance of laws but by a real personal relationship with God in faith and love.

Psalm 49 makes it clear that sacrifices are not meant to meet God's needs (as though food was offered to satisfy his hunger!) but rather to meet the human need to express to God our love and gratitude and worship.

Prayerful Ponderings

'The God of gods, the Lord, has spoken and summoned the earth, from the rising of the sun to its setting.'
This psalm is modelled on proceedings in a court of law. The judge is none other than God himself; he is presented as summoning witnesses from east to west, 'from the rising of the sun to its setting'. There is an air of suspense – though this is lost in the abridged version of the psalm we have today – for as yet it is not clear who is to be the accused in the dock. Incredibly, it is none of the pagan nations but rather God's own chosen people.

'I find no fault with your sacrifices, your offerings are always before me.'
In itself sacrifice – and there was no shortage of such 'offerings' in Israel – is an appropriate and acceptable way of worshipping God; and yet there must be no illusion about it: if it amounts to nothing more than mindless ritualism it is worse than useless. (We dare not forget that the same stricture applies even to the sacrifice of the Mass: if we are to benefit from this supreme act of worship, we must be something more than idle spectators who merely fulfil the letter of the law.)

'Were I hungry, I would not tell you, for I own the world and all it holds. Do you think I eat the flesh of bulls, or drink the blood of goats?'

God is sovereignly Other, completely independent of his creatures, and so they must not imagine that they can nourish him by such pathetic food-parcels as 'the flesh of bulls' or 'the blood of goats'. The fact is that he is Lord and Master of 'the world and all it holds'. (We may be in no danger of falling into such naive misunderstandings, yet we too have the lifelong task of appreciating ever more deeply God's complete otherness, his total independence of us and anything we might do for him.)

'Pay your sacrifice of thanksgiving to God and render him your votive offerings. Call on me in the day of distress. I will free you and you shall honour me.'

So it is indeed right and acceptable that 'sacrifice' and 'offerings' be made to God, provided that they reflect a genuine relationship with God, a relationship which does not arise from any notion that we can treat God as an equal, still less as a needy colleague, but rather from the realisation that it is he who responds to our cries in times of 'distress', he who sets us 'free', while it is our task to 'honour' him.

'I will show God's salvation to the upright.'

This verse, which serves as the refrain to today's responsorial psalm, comes from the end of the psalm, after God has indicted the 'wicked', those who fail to live up to the covenant. However, the final words are words not of condemnation but of instruction, and even of encouragement. 'God's salvation' is for 'the upright' and, in the light of what has gone before, as well as of what has been said in the other readings, 'the upright' person is the one whose worship stems from a right relationship with God and our fellow men and women.

LET US PRAY: *Almighty God, ruler of all the earth, we thank you for enabling us to share in the infinitely pleasing sacrifice which your Son Jesus offered on Calvary; may we who are so honoured live lives that show that our worship is genuine worship 'in spirit and in truth'.*

Eleventh Sunday in Ordinary Time

In the first reading (Exodus 19:2-6) Moses addresses the people, who have narrowly escaped genocide in Egypt and are now gathered in the wilderness near Sinai. He assures them that, if only they obey the God who rescued them, he will enter into a covenant with them so that they become '[his] very own', 'a kingdom of priests, a consecrated nation'.

The gospel (Matthew 9:36-10:8) shows that initially Jesus confined his ministry to the chosen people; it distressed him that they were 'like sheep without a shepherd' and so he commissioned the twelve apostles – their number reminiscent of the twelve tribes of Israel – to proclaim the good news of the kingdom.

However, the good news was never intended for Israel alone. As Paul makes clear in a letter addressed to Gentiles as well as Jews (Romans 5:6-11), 'at his appointed time' Jesus died for us all. His death has reconciled us to God and so we are invited to belong to his flock, to become a priestly people.

Psalm 99 is a processional song of praise which would accompany the people as they came to the Temple. In fact one of its verses, though it does not appear in today's responsorial psalm, speaks specifically of going 'within his [temple] gates' and 'entering his [temple] courts'. The psalm also gives reasons for worshipping God: first, because we are in his presence; second, because we are 'his people', 'the sheep of his flock'; and, third, because 'his merciful love' is never-fading.

Prayerful Ponderings

'Cry out with joy to the Lord, all the earth. Serve the Lord with gladness. Come before him, singing for joy.'

It would be hard to find a more encouraging call to worship. We are invited to come in a spirit of 'gladness' and 'singing for joy' (like Mary in her Magnificat), because we are coming 'before him', that is to say, 'into God's own presence'. And 'all the earth', the whole of humanity, is invited to join us. In his apostolic letter 'The Lord's Day', Pope John Paul II insists that Sunday ought to be a day of joy because true Christian joy does not depend upon the changing circumstances of life but upon the unchanging love of God so clearly manifested in the death and resurrection of his Son.

Together with the exuberant invitation, there is also the reminder that we come not simply for our own satisfaction but to 'serve'. As Israel's escape from Pharaoh set them free to serve the Lord, so the redeeming work of Christ has empowered us so that, in the words of Zechariah, 'we might serve him in holiness and justice all the days of our life'.

'Know that he, the Lord, is God. He made us, we belong to him, we are his people, the sheep of his flock.'

If the realisation that we stand in God's presence is a first reason for worship, this verse adds a second: the fact that the One whom Israel called 'Lord' (*Yahweh*) is in fact the only God and, as we Christians might add, the Father of our Lord Jesus Christ. The consequences are stated in a series of brief statements:

- 'he made us' – the reference is not simply to creation but to the whole history of salvation: beginning with the choice of Abraham and his descendants, continuing with the Exodus, the choice of Israel, the covenant – and reaching its climax in the saving work of our Lord Jesus Christ. All that we have, all that we are, is of his making; what more natural than that we should praise and thank him? Nor is his 'making' of us over: not only is he keeping us in being, he is also gradually transforming us into the likeness of his Son;
- 'we belong to him' – we are totally his possession: a truth made known to Israel at Sinai (see today's first reading) and to us through the whole mission of Jesus;
- 'we are his people' – at the Second Vatican Council the Church was described as 'the People of God', a priestly, royal and prophetic people;
- 'the sheep of his flock' – this image, which runs through today's Mass, is of course only another way of saying that we are the people of God, his 'very own'. That too was taken up by Vatican II in its description of the Church.

'Indeed, how good is the Lord, eternal his merciful love. He is faithful from age to age.'

This line may well have been a liturgical formula that the priests would proclaim at the beginning of a temple service. Our worship is based not only on the fact that we are in his presence, or that 'he made us [and] we belong to him' (see previous verses), but also on the fact that he is a God of goodness, unending 'love' and abiding faithfulness. His goodness is not simply a passing show of concern for us, but rather a permanent disposition in our regard. Taken all in all, this ancient hymn of praise still serves as a precious way of expressing our gratitude and worship.

LET US PRAY: *Lord, with pride but also with humility, we acknowledge that we are your people, your flock; we pray that we may fulfil our priestly task of worshipping you and of spreading the good news to others so that the work you entrusted to the Twelve may continue in the world.*

Twelfth Sunday in Ordinary Time

The first reading (Jeremiah 20:10-13) comes from one of Jeremiah's 'confessions', passages in which the prophet pours out his heart before God, telling of the enemies that threaten him from within and without. Yet nothing can make him lose confidence in 'the Lord [who] is at my side, a mighty hero'.

In the gospel (Matthew 10:26-33) Jesus reminds the Twelve that they, like the prophets of old, will have much to suffer; yet, he bids them, 'do not be afraid', the Father's tender care will never desert them; 'every hair on your head has been counted'.

The second reading (Romans 5:12-15) resonates with the others for Paul speaks of 'sin' and 'death', the twin evils that seem to threaten our happiness; yet he assures us that through the coming of the Second Adam, Jesus, we have the answer to sin and death. We need not fear.

Psalm 68 is the cry of anguish of a person in mortal danger. Despite the obvious distress that is being experienced, the psalmist has confidence in God and '[his] great love' and so will not fear.

Prayerful Ponderings

'It is for you that I suffer taunts, that shame covers my face, that I have become a stranger to my brothers, an alien to my own mother's sons.'

This gives a powerful picture of the torments suffered by the psalmist: there is no means of knowing their precise nature, but that doesn't really matter. It is enough that we know that they involved 'taunts' and insults, which brought with them feelings of 'shame', and there was also a sense of alienation from family and dear ones, even from 'my own mother's sons'. It is difficult to know why God should be blamed for this state of affairs – 'It is for you that I suffer' – but at least we might learn a valuable lesson from it: we need not be afraid in prayer to air our grievances against God, to tell him how upset we are and even that we feel he has let us down (if that is, in fact, how we see things). Our God is big enough to take that sort of thing in his stride!

'I burn with zeal for your house and taunts against you fall on me.'

The opening phrase, 'I burn with zeal for your house', is the first of eight passages in Psalm 68 – though only this one appears in today's responsorial psalm – which are at least indirectly referred to in the New Testament. This one is quoted in John (2:17), after Jesus had made 'a whip of cords' and driven out of the Temple the money-changers and those who sold cattle, sheep and doves, because they were 'making my Father's house a market-place'; it was as though their insulting behaviour towards the Father's house ricocheted onto himself.

As already explained, we do not know the original circumstances in which this psalm was sung, but it seems as though the psalmist's total commitment to the Temple and its worship has earned the 'taunts' of others, and it is a far from pleasant experience.

'This is my prayer to you, my prayer for your favour. In your great love, answer me, O God, with your help that never fails: Lord, answer, for your love is kind; in your compassion turn towards me.'

In the hour of distress it is to God that the psalmist turns in prayer, pleading with him for his 'favour', boldly proclaiming God's unfailing 'help' and 'great love'. The refrain is: 'In your great love, answer me, O God'; it is on that firm foundation that the whole psalm rests. God's love is 'kind', is gentle, is compassionate; it is that love which leads him to 'turn towards' us when we pray.

'The poor when they see it will be glad and God-seeking hearts will revive; for the Lord listens to the needy and does not spurn his servants in their chains.'

A favourable answer to the psalmist's plea will be a source of confidence to 'the poor' – which in this context seems to mean anyone who is distressed – and 'God-seeking hearts' will revive, will breathe again with relief: they will know that their trust is not in vain, that God does indeed 'listen to the needy', that he never abandons 'his servants' in their times of suffering.

'Let the heavens and the earth give him praise, the sea and all its living creatures.'

Finally, the psalmist confidently invites not only fellow-worshippers to join in the thanksgiving and 'praise' to God, but the whole universe – 'the heavens and the earth' alike – and even 'the sea' with its myriad of 'living creatures'.

LET US PRAY: *Today, Lord, you teach us that in our times of trial we are to cry out to you with complete trust in your unshakeable love; but may we also be ready to offer you our praise and our thanks for the unfailing help that we receive from your hands.*

Thirteenth Sunday in Ordinary Time

Today's gospel (Matthew 10:37-42) makes it clear that the true following of Christ – and this applies to every Christian, not just to priests and religious! – is a costly business. He must come first in our affections – if need be, before parents or children – following him involves 'the cross', even to the extent of risking one's life for his sake. However, those who help his friends never go unrewarded, though they do no more than offer them 'a cup of cold water'.

The second reading (Romans 6:3-4, 8-11) reminds us that, having been baptised into Christ's death, we must be dead to sin and 'live a new life', 'life with God'. It is only in the power made available to us in that new life that we can hope to fulfil the demands of discipleship.

As an example of the way God rewards those who welcome his messengers, there is the charming story of the first reading (2 Kings 4:8-11, 14-16): the prophet Elisha, who had always received hospitality in the home of a childless woman, is able to reassure her that she will soon have a child of her own.

If at times discipleship seems daunting, there is no mistaking the joy and the enthusiasm and the rejoicing in the Lord of those who sing Psalm 88, from which today's responsorial psalm is taken. In its original context the psalm, or at any rate that part of it which is our concern today, centred upon God's promise to David's dynasty of a throne for ever.

Prayerful Ponderings

'I will sing for ever of your love, O Lord; through all ages my mouth will proclaim your truth.'
Discipleship is not so much a matter of obeying instructions as of loving a person, the One who first loved us. In a way the psalmist could never have guessed, we can look forward to singing of God's love not merely 'through all ages' but literally 'for ever': it will be our joyous occupation for eternity. 'I will sing for ever of your love, O Lord' is the refrain of today's responsorial psalm and was one of St Teresa of Avila's favourite quotations from the Psalter.

'Of this I am sure, that your love lasts for ever, that your truth is firmly established as the heavens.'
This verse singles out the two characteristic attributes of the God of the covenant. He has entered into a special relationship with his people, and they can always rely upon, first, his 'love' (*hesed*) and, second, his 'truth' (*emuna*). The second word (from which 'Amen' is derived) means not so much truth as steadfastness, fidelity; the first has been translated in a variety of ways: fidelity, mercy, steadfast love, goodness, loving kindness. Between them they point to the utterly reliable love and merciful kindness which God has shown to his people and upon which they can always depend. For us who belong to the New Covenant, the reasons for trusting to his 'love' and 'truth' are still more powerful.

'Happy the people who acclaim such a king, who walk, O Lord, in the light of your face, who find their joy every day in your name, who make your justice the source of their bliss.'
There is joy and happiness for 'people who acclaim such a king'; the reference may be to the cry 'The Lord reigns', with which the congregation would acknowledge the kingship of God. To have such a king is to be able to 'walk... in the light'; to rejoice daily 'in [his] name' and in all that he means to us; and to find delight in the 'justice' of all his dealings.

'For it is you, O Lord, who are the glory of their strength; it is by your favour that our might is exalted.'
The sentiments of the previous line are now repeated: God himself is the source of the 'strength' in which people find 'glory'; and so they thrill with joy, they find inspiration in his graciousness and love.

'For our ruler is in the keeping of the Lord; our king in the keeping of the Holy One of Israel.'
For the first singers of this psalm, 'our ruler' and 'our king' referred of course to the Davidic king of the day, but for us Christians they speak of the true Davidic king, the one to whom all the successors of King David pointed, the one whose birth was foretold in these words: 'You shall call his name Jesus... and the Lord God will give him the throne of his father David... and of his kingdom there will be no end' (Luke 1:31-33).

LET US PRAY: *Lord, we rejoice to be disciples of Jesus Christ our Lord; in him, all your promises are fulfilled, your unfailing love made manifest and your covenant renewed. May we walk in the light of his presence, find joy in his care for us, and one day meet him face to face in that kingdom of which there is no end.*

Fourteenth Sunday in Ordinary Time

Today's first reading (Zechariah 9:9-10) visualises the arrival in his city of the Messiah King: he comes not proudly on a warhorse but humbly on a donkey. His very appearance invites rejoicing for it heralds an era of peace.

The responsorial psalm, taken from Psalm 144, rejoices in the Great King, God himself, and in the compassion and faithfulness he shows to all.

What the psalmist could never have known, the gospel (Matthew 11:25-30) reveals when it presents Jesus as the fulfilment of Zechariah's prophecy. It is he who will establish a kingdom of peace and it is he, to whom the Father has entrusted everything, who alone reveals God to humankind, though it is a revelation that only the humble, the 'mere children', are able to understand.

St Paul (Romans 8:9, 11-13) insists that to 'live spiritually' is to belong to Christ and be filled with his Spirit. It is a life of peace where the God of compassion reigns as King.

Prayerful Ponderings

'I will give you glory, O God my King, I will bless your name for ever. I will bless you day after day and praise your name for ever.'

This psalm holds a special place in the Church's liturgy: it appears on no fewer than half a dozen occasions among the responsorial psalms of various Sundays. From the outset it is clear that its purpose is to 'give glory' and to 'bless', not merely 'day after day' but 'for ever'. The object of the praise is of course God himself, or, more precisely, God in his role as great and universal 'King'. There is something moving in the realisation that at the end of each verse of this psalm, as we take up the refrain 'I will bless your name for ever, O God my King', we are doing what our Jewish and Christian forebears have done down the centuries; but we are also helping to ensure that the blessing and praising of the King will indeed go on 'for ever'.

'The Lord is kind and full of compassion, slow to anger and abounding in love. How good is the Lord to all, compassionate to all his creatures.'

Now come the reasons for the praise: he is a King whose outstanding characteristics are kindness, compassion, slowness to anger and abounding love. This compassionate love of his extends 'to all his creatures' and especially, as we shall see, to the downcast and the needy. According to Brueggemann, one of the finest modern commentators on the Psalms, here we have a vision which reflects 'Israel's oldest theological assertion about God'; even before he came to be recognised as King, he was saluted and praised as a God, passionately and limitlessly in love with his people, his covenant partners. It need hardly be added that the coming of Jesus has served only to highlight all that was understood of God in the past.

'All your creatures shall thank you, O Lord, and your friends shall repeat their blessing. They shall speak of the glory of your reign and declare your might, O God.'
The repetition of the word 'all' throughout the psalm – 'compassionate to all', 'all his creatures', 'all his words', 'all his deeds', 'all who fall' – serves to emphasise the universality of God's loving concern. And so the whole of creation is invited to express its thanks, a 'blessing' that will be taken up by his 'friends', who will go on to proclaim 'the glory of [his] reign' and the greatness of his 'deeds'.

'The Lord is faithful in all his words and loving in all his deeds. The Lord supports all who fall and raises all who are bowed down.'
Everything about this great God, whether it be 'his words' or 'his deeds', conspires to bear witness to his faithfulness and his love. Nowhere is this more evident than in his concern for 'all who fall' under the burdens of life or of sinfulness, and 'all who are bowed down', those bent double by frailty and weakness.

LET US PRAY: *We rejoice, we bless and we give thanks that you, O Lord, are our faithful and compassionate King, and that in the lowliness of your Son Jesus you have revealed yourself to us. May we always be your humble and faithful servants.*

Fifteenth Sunday
in Ordinary Time

Isaiah (55:10-11) likens the effectiveness of 'the rain and snow', which automatically water the earth and make it fertile, to the effectiveness of God's word, which is always successful in what it is sent to do.

The gospel parable (Matthew 13:1-23) also speaks of the effectiveness of God's word, but with an important difference of emphasis: though that word, like a seed that is sown, is unfailing in its power, yet its effectiveness also depends upon the human response that is given it.

The responsorial psalm comes from the latter part of Psalm 64, a hymn of praise for the blessings of the annual harvest, and uses as its refrain words from the parable of the sower.

The second reading (Romans 8:18-23) also speaks of harvest-time: already we have received 'the first-fruits of the Spirit', but, with the rest of creation, we groan as we await the final harvest; anything we suffer in the meantime cannot be compared with the glory to come.

Prayerful Ponderings

'Some seed fell into rich soil, and produced its crop.'
This refrain, taken directly from today's gospel, puts us in mind of the overarching theme of today's readings, and in particular of the gospel parable. Every seed has within itself the potential to produce much fruit, but its effectiveness is also dependent upon its being received into 'rich soil'. Our Lord's prayer at the Last Supper was that his disciples might 'bear much fruit'. Perhaps on this Sunday we ought to be asking him to make us into rich, welcoming soil for his word.

'You care for the earth, give it water, you fill it with riches. Your river in heaven brims over to provide its grain.'
God is envisaged as a farmer who has real 'care for the earth'; he waters it faithfully and so enables it to be filled 'with riches'. 'You visit' might be a more accurate translation of the Hebrew phrase rendered 'you care'; visiting is a typical biblical way of expressing God's intervention in time of need. With poetic fancy the psalmist pictures as the source of all this fruitfulness a mighty heavenly river whose inexhaustible waters overflow its banks to re-create the earth and 'provide its grain'.

'And thus you provide for the earth; you drench its furrows, you level it, soften it with showers, you bless its growth.'
This verse takes up again the word 'provide', as if to emphasise the

generosity of God's provision for 'the earth'. And again there is emphasis on water, that blessed gift to parched land, soaking the hard clots of 'its furrows', and levelling the ground after the softening 'showers'. It is all a divine gift which results in fruitful 'growth' and abundant crops.

'You crown the year with your goodness. Abundance flows in your steps, in the pastures of the wilderness it flows.'
The whole 'year' through is likened to a king or queen, crowned by God with the jewels of his 'abundance'. The sense of the final sentence, or at any rate the idea at the back of the mind of its poet-author, seems to be that God's chariot wheels (rather than his 'steps') cross the earth, even the barren 'wilderness', dispensing fertility like largesse as they go.

'The hills are girded with joy, the meadows covered with flocks, the valleys are decked with wheat. They shout for joy, yes, they sing.'
The poet's eye sees the whole of nature adorned with festive apparel: the 'hills' joyously clad in green grass, 'the meadows' adorned 'with flocks' and even the 'valleys' attired in a garb of golden 'wheat'. And the poet's ear hears all renewed creation singing and crying 'for joy'. This is the kind of poem which must touch the heart, especially of the town-dweller; and yet the wonders of nature are but a symbol of the still greater wonders that the Lord works in the hearts of those who are open to receive him.

LET US PRAY: *Lord, forgive us for our past failures to thank you for all the good things that come to us through your hands. Help us to be ever more grateful, and make us into fertile land where the seed of your grace may quickly take root and bear lasting fruit to the glory of your name.*

Sixteenth Sunday in Ordinary Time

God's mercy and compassion are the theme running through today's readings. The excerpt from Wisdom (12:13, 16-19), a book written about the middle of the first century BC, speaks of God's universal care. It is a sign of his strength, and a source of hope to us all, that he is 'mild in judgement'.

Psalm 85 is largely composed of traditional formulas about God, many of which are to be found elsewhere in the Psalter. They provide the basis for an appeal for help: in the midst of his troubles the psalmist time and again acknowledges the greatness of God's mercy.

The main parable of the gospel (Matthew 13:24-43) compares the kingdom of God to a mixed crop of wheat and weeds (darnel) – a shrewd picture of the ambiguities and complexities of the actual situation in the Church. At the same time it directs our attention to God's patience, his slowness to pass judgement. There is time for repentance, thanks to his mercy, but in the end a choice must be made.

Paul (Romans 8:26-27) is at least indirectly referring to God's compassion when he assures us that in our prayers, even when we scarcely know what to say, the Holy Spirit himself is with us, giving expression to what is beyond words.

Prayerful Ponderings

'O Lord, you are good and forgiving, full of love to all who call.'
The first part of this sentence serves as the refrain for today's
responsorial psalm. It is a statement of faith, a confession of belief
in God's nature; their own experience had taught God's people that
he is 'good and forgiving'. An interesting feature of this psalm (see
below for further examples), though unfortunately it does not
show up in translation, is the repeated emphasis on the word 'you',
in relation to God. It is the psalmist's way of saying that, however
difficult things may be, at least we can rely upon you, our God. His
universal 'love' is especially available to those who have faith
enough to 'call' upon his help.

'Give heed, O Lord, to my prayer and attend to the sound of
my voice.'
After the confession of faith in God's readiness to respond to those
who seek his help, there comes, naturally enough, the psalmist's
own prayer. It's a prayer that God will listen to him, will hear 'the
sound of my voice' (just as parents readily recognise the voice of
their own child) – and be ready to reply.

'All the nations shall come to adore you and glorify your
name, O Lord: for you are great and do marvellous deeds, you
who alone are God.'

Beyond God's willingness to help, lies his power to do so. It is a power which arises from the fact that there is no deity like him; that is why 'all the nations' – in the psalmist's day every nation had its own local deity – will 'come' to pay honour and worship to the Lord's 'name'. The simple fact is that he is beyond compare in his greatness and in all his 'marvellous deeds'. And this leads to a another emphatic 'you' and a second statement of faith: 'you... alone are God'.

'But you, God of mercy and compassion, slow to anger, O Lord, abounding in love and truth, turn and take pity on me.' This is the third emphatic 'you' in today's psalm and again it introduces a statement of faith, perhaps the best known in the Old Testament. It is first recorded in Exodus 34:6 when God, in response to Moses' request, reveals his divine attributes, especially those which concern his faithful love, his 'compassion', his abiding 'mercy'. The same formula appears again in other psalms (for example Psalm 102:8) as well as in the books of Joel (2:13) and Jonah (4:2). The author of this psalm uses it as the grounds upon which God must surely hear the appeal that he is making this day.

LET US PRAY: *Lord God, with the psalmist we profess our faith in your patience and compassion and faithful love. Help us to be slow to judge others, remembering always that the dividing line between good and evil runs through the heart of each one of us.*

Seventeenth Sunday in Ordinary Time

Treasure is very much on the agenda of today's readings. Assured by God that he can have whatever he desires, King Solomon chooses not the obvious treasure – riches or power – but rather that of a wise and discerning heart, so that he will be able to rule his people in accordance with the mind of God (1 Kings 3:5, 7-12).

Treasure, hidden treasure, also appears in the gospel (Matthew 13:44-52), a treasure so precious that it's worth selling all one has to take possession of it. To lose the treasure, which is nothing less than Christ himself and his kingdom, is to become like the dregs from a dragnet which can only be cast aside as worthless.

The verses taken from Psalm 118 indicate that the glad acceptance of God's Law, the whole-hearted adoption of his teaching, is more precious than any treasure.

Meanwhile Paul (Romans 8:28-30) insists that God, who has already begun the work of salvation in us, will continue to be faithful, turning everything to the good for those who love him.

Prayerful Ponderings

'Lord, how I love your law!'
These words, summing up as they do the whole thrust of the responsorial psalm, serve as an ideal refrain. For the pious Jew, the word 'law' meant much more than rules and regulations, though of course it did include them: its primary meaning was 'instruction'; it came to denote sacred Scripture, its first five books in particular, and, ultimately, it included God's entire revelation, a revelation which was seen to be an expression of his love. For the Christian, the law is personified in Jesus Christ, who came, as he explained, 'to fulfil the law and the prophets' (Matthew 5:17); he himself is the fullest possible revelation of the Father: 'to have seen me', he says, 'is to have seen the Father' (John 14:9); his words and the example of his life provide perfect instruction on how we are to live if we are to enter the kingdom (see today's gospel). As we pray this psalm it might be helpful each time we come across the word 'law' (and its equivalents) to think of Jesus, the living Word of God and the fulfilment of the law.

'My part, I have resolved, O Lord, is to obey your word. The law from your mouth means more to me than silver and gold.'
Love of God is manifested in whole-hearted acceptance of his will, in readiness to listen to his 'word', in welcoming the revelation that comes to us through his Son Jesus. That revelation is a treasure more precious 'than silver and gold' for it leads to the kingdom.

'Let your love be ready to console me by your promise to your servant. Let your love come to me and I shall live, for your law is my delight. That is why I love your commands more than finest gold. That is why I rule my life by your precepts: I hate false ways.'

God's 'law', his revelation, his commandments, above all his Son, are pledge and promise of his 'love'. It is a love which brings consolation, which is life-giving and a source of 'delight'. So it is that the psalmist and, still more, Christians are happy to call themselves his 'servant', and to boast that they have a 'love' for God's 'commands' greater than their love for 'finest gold'. His commands are in truth a treasure, a perfect rule of life and a powerful safeguard against following the many 'false ways' that are enticingly set before us.

'Your will is wonderful indeed; therefore I obey it. The unfolding of your word gives light and teaches the simple.'

It may not always seem that way, but, given that God is good, that his love for us is so immense that he gave his only Son and that he never has anything but our best interests at heart, his 'will' must be 'wonderful indeed'. It would be the height of folly on our part to imagine that we could lay hold of true happiness any other way. His 'word' brings 'light' into our lives, it brings wisdom and instruction to those who, in Jesus' words, have become as 'little children'.

LET US PRAY: *Lord God, on this day we wish to give you thanks for all your blessings but above all for the gift of your Son Jesus, who is the fulfilment of the law, the surest revelation of yourself, and our most precious treasure.*

Eighteenth Sunday in Ordinary Time

No material food or drink can satisfy our deepest yearnings. In the first reading (Isaiah 55:1-3) God gives the assurance, through his prophet, that the people newly returned from exile can be confident that their needs will be met. The 'water' for thirsty souls will be given free, the 'corn, wine and milk' for hungry hearts will be made available without charge.

It is this generosity of God towards his creatures that is reflected in the passage from Psalm 144 which makes up the responsorial psalm for today's Mass.

Paul (Romans 8:35, 37-39) also insists that something more than food is needed if we are to be fully alive: we need to be loved and know that we are loved. In fact we have the assurance of such love, the overflowing love of Jesus, a love so great that there is nothing, not even death itself, that can separate us from it.

In the gospel (Matthew 14:13-21) we are given an example of this love in Jesus' abundant provision of food for a great crowd of hungry people, but he makes provision in a way that hints at the free gift, the food and drink precious beyond price, that he will offer us in the Eucharist.

Prayerful Ponderings

'The Lord is kind and full of compassion, slow to anger, abounding in love.'
As has been mentioned before, this sentence, which comes almost word for word from God's self-revelation at Mount Sinai (Exodus 34:6), appears many times in Scripture. It is as fine an expression of the faith of the Jewish people as is to be found. It summarises all that we learn about God's nature from the pages of the Old Testament. He is – and today's readings confirm this description – 'kind', filled with a 'compassion' like that of a mother for her child; not easily roused to 'anger', he simply overflows with 'love', with steadfast faithfulness.

'How good is the Lord to all, compassionate to all his creatures.'
His goodness is universal and his compassion reaches out not only to people but to the whole of creation, 'all his creatures'. The whole of creation can be regarded as his gift to us, yet he relies upon us not to abuse it but rather to treat it with respect. All who pray this psalm should be 'friends of the earth', above all because the raw material, so to say, of the Eucharist comes from his inanimate creation – bread and wine, 'fruits of the earth and work of human hands'.

'The eyes of all creatures look to you and you give them their food in due time.'
The poet-psalmist visualises all God's creatures looking up to him

expectantly, rather like a pet animal that keeps an eye on its master at feeding time, confident that he will provide it with 'food'. As Jesus himself was to teach us, the Father feeds the birds of the air, without their having to reap or sow; similarly, he clothes the lilies of the fields in their glorious raiment, without their having to toil or spin. And the lesson to be drawn is that our trust in God ought to be so much firmer for we are of much greater value in the Father's sight than birds or flowers (Matthew 6:25-30).

'You open wide your hand, grant the desires of all who live.'
The response to the psalm is a slight variation on this line: 'O Lord' is added and 'our desires' replaces the more general 'the desires of all who live'. Once again we are put in mind of the sheer generosity of God, his open-handedness, his readiness to meet our deepest desires.

'The Lord is just in all his ways and loving in all his deeds. He is close to all who call him, call on him from their hearts.'
A final summary: in all that he does, our God acts justly and lovingly. It is for us, therefore, to trust him: he is always 'close' – closer than we are to ourselves, as St Augustine put it – but never more so than when we 'call on him' from a sincere heart.

LET US PRAY: *Lord God, we rejoice in you and we thank you because you are truly our Father, the giver of all good gifts, sustaining all creatures by your provident care but above all sustaining us, your children, in the Holy Eucharist. We offer our thanks through Christ our Lord.*

Nineteenth Sunday
in Ordinary Time

At a time when faith seems to be dead in Israel and his own life is in jeopardy from a pagan queen, Elijah the prophet (1 Kings 19:9, 11-13) journeys back to Mount Sinai where God had appeared to Moses. The Lord now appears to his disheartened prophet; but on this occasion not in fire or storm or earthquake but in a 'gentle breeze'.

The gospel (Matthew 14:22-33) tells a similar story, but with a richer significance: Jesus appears to the weary 'men in the boat' who are battling with a fierce headwind. Like the Lord's dispirited disciples of every era, they are slow to recognise his presence. But when at last the truth dawns – it is he who is actually walking in the midst of the stormy waters – they can only kneel in worship.

In the second reading (Romans 9:1-5) Paul expresses the grief he feels that his own people have failed to recognise God's presence in the person of Jesus Christ; he would willingly forgo anything so long as they finally come to the truth about Christ.

The verses taken from Psalm 84, today's responsorial psalm, might have been spoken by Elijah for they express a great longing to see God's mercy and salvation, and a readiness to listen to God with open ear.

Prayerful Ponderings

'Let us see, O Lord, your mercy and give us your saving help.'
Like Elijah on Mount Sinai, like the disciples on the Lake of Galilee, we long to experience the goodness of God and his 'saving help'. The earlier part of this psalm, which does not appear in today's Mass, suggests that originally the psalm was used by the exiles as they returned from Babylon to their devastated homeland; it is a plea that God who favoured them so richly in the past will favour them once more. We too may pray the psalm with similar sentiments: may the God who has shown us so much kindness in times gone by continue to show us his favour now and in the future.

'I will hear what the Lord God has to say, a voice that speaks of peace.'
An individual (notice the 'I'), perhaps a temple priest or prophet, acknowledges that what really matters is not that we get what we want from God but rather that we listen to what he 'has to say' to us. His 'voice' is one that forever 'speaks of peace'. Peace (*shalom*), which is used as a standard greeting, becomes so much more when spoken by God, not only because it indicates wholeness, harmony, complete well-being, but also because God's word is creative: he does not merely speak of peace, he creates it.

'His help is near for those who fear him and his glory will dwell in our land.'

The speaker of the previous verse promises his hearers that they will recognise that God's 'help' is already here, present in the midst, provided only that they hold him in reverential 'fear'. Despite the devastation they see all about them — the aftermath of the Babylonian invasion of fifty years before — God's 'glory', his very presence, is to take up its dwelling in the 'land'. When the exile began, God's glory departed from Israel (see Ezekiel 10:18-19), but now 'his glory' is set to return. Our Christian belief is that in a still more glorious way the Lord-made-flesh has come to dwell amongst us as one of us, in our world devastated by sin, and 'we have seen his glory... full of grace and truth' (John 1:14).

'Mercy and faithfulness have met; justice and peace have embraced. Faithfulness shall spring from the earth and justice look down from heaven.'

This verse is justly famous as a poetic expression of what God's salvation means. It means that we experience the combination of his 'mercy' (his steadfast love) and his 'faithfulness'; it means a harmony between earth and heaven, the conjunction of 'justice' (righteousness) and 'peace' (in the rich sense mentioned above).

'The Lord will make us prosper and our earth shall yield its fruit. Justice shall march before him and peace shall follow his steps.'

The outcome of the 'embrace' between mercy and faithfulness, justice and peace, is that 'the Lord' will bless us with prosperity, with a fruitful 'earth'. 'Justice', his saving mercy, is visualised as marching before him and 'peace' following in 'his [foot]steps'. This verse refers to a future happening; while Jesus proclaims that with his presence 'the kingdom of God is [already] close at hand' (Mark 1:15), yet it will not arrive in all its fullness until he comes again.

LET US PRAY: *Lord God, we are 'exiled children of Eve'; in the midst of the problems and difficulties of life, let us never lose sight of the fact that your Son, Jesus, has blessed us with his presence, has brought about our salvation, has won us a peace which is wonderful beyond all our imagining.*

Twentieth Sunday
in Ordinary Time

We take for granted the universality of the Church's mission. But in the days before Christ's coming, it was perhaps the exceptional person, such as the author of today's first reading (Isaiah 56:1, 6-7), who realised that the God of Israel was God of all the world and that therefore people of integrity could not be excluded from the community simply because they were 'foreigners'.

The author of Psalm 66 shares a similar vision for he prays that 'all the peoples' may come to praise the God of Israel.

The gospel (Matthew 15:21-28) seems to suggest that it was the persistence and wit of a pagan woman that brought Jesus himself to the realisation — being like us in all things but sin, he was a man of his time, he too had to learn — that his mission was not to be restricted to 'the lost sheep of the House of Israel'.

Paul in the second reading (Romans 11:13-15, 29-32) is aware of the opposite danger, that of Gentile Christians wishing to exclude Jews from the Church! He longs for Jews and Gentiles to be united, each bringing blessings to the other.

Prayerful Ponderings

'O God, be gracious and bless us and let your face shed its light upon us.'
The book of Numbers (6:24-26) records the formula used by Aaron and the priests of Israel when they wished to bless the people. They would say: 'The Lord bless you and keep you; the Lord make his face to shine upon you, and be gracious to you.' It's a formula which clearly lies behind the opening verse of this psalm. The psalm itself is a plea that God will show graciousness towards us, will 'bless' us. Another, more poetic, way of saying the same thing is to beg that God will let his 'face shed its light upon us'. Nothing could be more desirable than that God's face should light up with a smile as he gazes upon his people.

'So will your ways be known upon earth and all nations learn your saving help.'
However, the prayer is not as selfish as it might sound: the blessing of the people is seen as a bridgehead whereby God's 'ways' may come to be universally recognised and 'all nations learn', experience for themselves, his 'saving help'; and so join Israel in its worship.

'Let the nations be glad and exult for you rule the world with justice. With fairness you rule the peoples, you guide the nations on earth.'

Here it becomes even clearer that the blessing of Israel is meant to fan out to all 'the nations' so that they too may 'be glad and exult' in his universal 'rule'. It is a rule which brings guidance, but always in the spirit of 'justice' and 'fairness'.

'Let the peoples praise you, O God; let all the peoples praise you.' It's hardly surprising that this verse should be the response for today's psalm, because in fact in the psalm itself it serves as a type of chorus. It appears three times over, summing up again and again the psalm's major concern, that God's blessing should not be confined to Israel but should spread to all 'the peoples' so that they in their turn may 'praise' and worship God. The more we ponder this psalm, the more we are reminded of the opening words of Vatican II's Decree on the Missionary Activity of the Church: 'The pilgrim church is of its very nature missionary.'

'May God still give us his blessing till the ends of the earth revere him.'
Having prayed for the nations, the psalm returns to base, as it were, with the plea that God will continue to bless his people, but that that will result in his universal worship to 'the ends of the earth'. This psalm was surely composed in the light of God's promise to Abraham in Genesis 12:1-3, that all the families of the earth would be blessed in him, and of Isaiah 40-55, which proclaims that the salvation of Israel will be a revelation that the Lord reigns and will lead the families of people to praise him.

LET US PRAY: *Mindful that you, O God, are God of all peoples, we pray that we may do all in our power to ensure 'that in (Christ) all humankind may form but one family, one people of God'.*

Twenty-First Sunday in Ordinary Time

In the first reading (Isaiah 22:19-23) the Lord appoints a new royal official. He will receive a key – mention of his bearing it on his shoulder may be a reference to the actual investiture – as a symbol of his God-given authority, and God himself will 'drive him like a peg into a firm place'.

Is there perhaps at least an implicit reference in the gospel (Matthew 16:13-20) to the situation described in the first reading? Having confessed that Jesus is the 'Messiah, the Son of the living God', Peter is given the power of the keys and hailed as the cornerstone of the Church, with a new name to reflect his position. He, by God's grace, will be 'a peg [driven] into a firm place'.

Having devoted three chapters to explaining how God despite his call to the Gentiles remains faithful to his original choice of the Jewish people, Paul (Romans 11:33-36) bursts into a rapturous hymn of praise for God's plans and God's wisdom.

All genuine authority comes from God. The verses taken from Psalm 137 as today's responsorial psalm underline the fact that human authority is only safe when it is undergirded by God's love and power.

Prayerful Ponderings

'I thank you, Lord, with all my heart, you have heard the words of my mouth.'

The opening words of the psalm indicate that this is a song of thanksgiving and that it's uttered by an individual, though we have no means of knowing who he or she might be. It's equally clear that the reason for the thanksgiving is a prayer – 'the words of my mouth' – that has been heard.

'Before the angels I will bless you. I will adore before your holy temple.'

The thanksgiving, which takes the form of blessing and praising God, goes up to his 'holy temple': probably the reference is to the Temple in Jerusalem but possibly the holy temple of heaven itself is intended. In any case the worship takes place 'before the angels'. The word translated 'angels' literally means 'gods'. The sense may be that though other nations have their so-called 'gods', those 'divinities' can only be put to shame by what the God of Israel, the only God, has done for me; or perhaps – and this is probably the easiest way for us to understand it – the psalmist sees God surrounded by lesser beings, angels, as we would call them, and it is in their presence that he gives thanks.

'I thank you for your faithfulness and love which excel all we ever knew of you.'

While the precise reason for thanksgiving is not given, it is stated in general terms: it is the fact that God's 'faithfulness' and 'love' have been brought home in ways which 'excel' anything the psalmist had ever before experienced. There are times in life when we all catch a fresh glimpse of God's goodness; for a moment we experience a new and deeper appreciation of his goodness and love.

'On the day I called, you answered; you increased the strength of my soul.'

Once more we are told that the psalmist's prayer was 'answered' and the net outcome was a strengthening of soul. We may be disappointed that the precise nature of the prayer is not given, and yet there is a sense in which that is an advantage, for it means that this psalm is not 'tied down' to one specific event: it may be used in any situation in which we feel the need to raise our voice in thanksgiving.

'The Lord is high yet he looks on the lowly and the haughty he knows from afar.'

The glory of 'the Lord' consists in this: that though 'high', 'yet he looks', with tenderness and compassion, 'on the lowly'; he also 'knows', and, by implication, ignores, 'the haughty'. This radical claim for the Lord – that he is not the God of the high and mighty but of the lowly – has enormous implications, as will become clear in the life of Jesus of Nazareth. In the context of today's readings, it is a powerful reminder that those in positions of power will never achieve lasting success unless they are lowly of heart, aware of their total dependence on God.

'Your love, O Lord, is eternal, discard not the work of your hands.' This verse is an appropriate refrain for today's psalm, particularly in view of the previous verse: God's love is eternal, unfading, and that is why he will never 'discard', cast aside, those who are lowly enough to recognise that they are not self-made men and women but 'the work of [his] hands'.

LET US PRAY: *Creator God, we are in all truth the work of your hands, totally dependent upon you, completely indebted to you for all that we have received; teach us how to keep our hearts always humble and grateful, to the glory of your name.*

Twenty-Second Sunday in Ordinary Time

If Peter's faith won him the Lord's approval in last Sunday's gospel, in this week's it is disapproval that he earns for his attempt to dissuade the Lord from the path that leads to Calvary (Matthew 16:21-27). Jesus goes on to insist that all true followers of his must be prepared to embrace suffering.

Like Peter, Jeremiah (20:7-9) came to see how costly his prophetic mission would be, but confesses that he could not resist God's call: the Lord was too strong for him, he overwhelmed him.

Paul (Romans 12:1-2) shows that he, too, is aware of the costliness of Christian discipleship for he bids us offer our 'living bodies as a holy sacrifice, truly pleasing to God'.

While today's readings highlight the price of following the Lord, they also hint that the price is well worth paying. And this is brought to the fore in Psalm 62, today's responsorial psalm, which speaks so passionately of our desire for God and, by implication, for whatever the following of him may involve.

Prayerful Ponderings

'O God, you are my God, for you I long; for you my soul is thirsting.'
These burning words of the psalmist strike a chord in many hearts; they are an expression of our longing for God, who is not simply the God of people *en masse*, but 'my God', loving me and caring for me, as he cares for every other creature, as though I were the only person in the world. My desire for him can be likened to a tormenting thirst; he and he alone can slake my deepest desires. How appropriately this thirsting for God is used as the refrain for the responsorial psalm.

'My body pines for you like a dry, weary land without water.'
A striking feature of Hebrew poetry is 'parallelism', the practice of repeating the same idea in a slightly different way in succeeding lines. And so, just as 'my soul is thirsting' (see previous line) so also 'my body pines' for the Lord. It's a forcible way of saying that the poet's whole self is yearning for God; it has become like a piece of arid 'land', grown 'weary' and fruitless 'without water'. The psalmist waits longingly for God as the land 'pines' for a refreshing, life-giving downpour of rain.

'So I gaze on you in the sanctuary to see your strength and your glory.'

It is a longing and a yearning that brings the psalmist to 'the sanctuary' in Jerusalem, God's own dwelling place, with the confident hope that there he will be renewed by catching some glimpse of the 'strength' and 'glory' of God.

'For your love is better than life, my lips will speak your praise.'
This is an astonishing statement – 'your love' (*hesed*) is worth more to me than 'life' itself – it is the sentiment which has inspired every martyr. Indeed, it reflects the forceful language of Jeremiah who describes himself as being 'seduced', 'overpowered' by God (see today's first reading). But it is also an attitude which is shared in some measure by every Christian who within the circumstances of his or her own life strives always to put God first.

'So I will bless you all my life, in your name I will lift up my hands.'
A God who is so dear to us is a God whose praise will be constantly upon our lips, a God whom all our life through we will 'bless' with worship and thanksgiving, a God to whom we will 'lift up [our] hands' in prayer.

'My soul shall be filled as with a banquet, my mouth shall praise you with joy.'
The worship of such a God will bring its own reward: the psalmist speaks of it in terms of a 'banquet' that sates our hunger; the 'praise' of such a God brings its own unique 'joy'.

'For you have been my help; in the shadow of your wings I rejoice. My soul clings to you; your right hand holds me fast.'
The psalmist is conscious that God has always 'been my help'; it is

as though he has been for ever kept safe 'in the shadow of [his] wings'; we are reminded of our Lord's sad words over Jerusalem when he speaks of the way he would so much have loved to gather the people of that city 'as a hen gathers her brood under her wings', but they would not (Luke 13:34). Like the psalmist, our aim is to 'cling' to God, in bad times as in good, confident always that his own 'right hand holds [us] fast'.

LET US PRAY: *Lord, you know the deep yearning for you in the depths of our hearts; let us never grow weary of raising our hearts to you in prayer and praise; and may we never doubt that your strong arms are about us and your right hand holds us fast.*

Twenty-Third Sunday in Ordinary Time

At a time when the superpower Babylon was threatening the whole of the Near East, sentries were posted to give warning of the enemies' approach. In today's first reading (Ezekiel 33:7-9) the prophet Ezekiel compares himself to such a sentry, whose task it is to give warning to those who persist in wickedness of the consequences of their actions.

The prophet's words are a foreshadowing of our Lord's teaching in the gospel (Matthew 18:15-20): we have a fraternal duty to do what we can when a brother's or sister's behaviour is a threat to the community.

Paul (Romans 13:8-10) indicates the basis for the gospel message when he speaks about 'the debt of mutual love' which we owe each other in the Christian community.

The theme of listening runs through the readings: listening to the prophet, listening to a brother or sister in the Christian community, listening to the Church. The verses, and in particular the refrain, of Psalm 94 pick up the idea of listening to the voice of God.

Prayerful Ponderings

'Come, ring out our joy to the Lord; hail the rock who saves us.' This psalm holds a unique place in the Church's liturgy; from earliest times it has been the very first psalm to be prayed each day in the Prayer of the Church, the Divine Office. A new day has begun and we are invited to take part in this hymn of praise, to 'come' into the Lord's presence in a spirit of 'joy' and to 'hail' in worship the God who is the 'rock' of our salvation. It is especially at Mass that we answer that call: we come with joy, we come to worship, we come to acknowledge the Lord and his saving sacrifice.

'Let us come before him, giving thanks, with songs let us hail the Lord.'
Again the invitation to 'come' into the Lord's presence is heard; this time we are invited to approach him in a spirit of gratitude, the appropriate spirit for the worship which is above all a Eucharist, a giving thanks. Once more, we are to 'hail' him, but this time 'with songs'; music has always played a significant part in the worship of God; indeed, what are the psalms themselves but songs whether of praise or of petition?

'Come in; let us bow and bend low; let us kneel before the God who made us...'
This verse gives us a glimpse of what worship was like in the world

of the psalmists: they and their contemporaries worshipped God not only with mind and heart but also with their bodies. They would 'bow', 'bend low' and 'kneel' before their Creator God. Each of the verbs suggests that by their actions they strove to lower themselves before God, rather in the way that Muslims today bow down to say their prayers, and for much the same reason: to show their submission (which is what 'Muslim' means) to God who is their Maker.

'...for he is our God and we the people who belong to his pasture, the flock that is led by his hand.'
However, this Creator God is also a Good Shepherd; he has a care for each individual member of his 'flock', he knows each of them personally, leads each of them in his or her unique path. With the coming of Christ it has been revealed that the love and devotion of our Good Shepherd leads him to lay down his life for his sheep (John 10).

'O that today you would listen to his voice!'
But now the time has come to 'listen' to the Lord, not in the sense that listening must now replace worship but rather in the sense that listening – in Scripture 'to listen' usually has the connotation of obeying, of putting into practice what you hear – is itself part of worship. He speaks to us in many ways – through the events of life, through the example of others, through the teaching of the Church and, above all, through the inspired words of the Bible.

‘"Harden not your hearts as at Meribah, as on that day at Massah in the desert when your fathers put me to the test; when they tried me, though they saw my work."'

This verse is a good example of what we often meet in Scripture: the advice to learn from the past (see 1 Corinthians 10:6). 'Meribah' (dispute) and 'Massah' (testing) are two place names (see Exodus 17:1-7 and Numbers 20:1-13), which are for ever associated with Israel's disputing with the Lord in the desert and putting him to the test. We must ensure that we do not 'harden our hearts', do not allow them to become deaf to the word of God.

LET US PRAY: *Amidst the distractions and bustle of everyday life, help us, Lord, to be alert in listening for your voice and generous in responding to it.*

Twenty-Fourth Sunday in Ordinary Time

Writing in the second century before Christ, Sirach, the author of the book of Ecclesiasticus (27:30–28:7), speaks of the dangers of the spirit of vengeance. 'Forgive your neighbour', he urges, 'and when you pray, your sins will be forgiven.'

The gospel (Matthew 18:21–35) reinforces the lesson of the first reading. Peter thought he was being generous when he suggested that we should be willing to forgive seven times, but Jesus' reply is that we must forgive seventy-seven times – so often that we lose count! And he illustrates the point with the parable of the man who, having been pardoned a huge debt, was unwilling to pardon a trifling one.

If, as St Paul teaches (Romans 14:7–9), we belong not to ourselves but to the Lord, it is hardly surprising that we are called upon to behave like the Lord in our dealings with others.

Some verses taken from Psalm 102 supply us with today's responsorial psalm, verses which highlight the endless compassion and mercy of God.

Prayerful Ponderings

'The Lord is compassion and love, slow to anger and rich in mercy.' This summary of God's attributes, revealed to Moses (Exodus 34:6), might be described as Israel's Credo, the belief by which the people lived. The remainder of the psalm is an unfolding of its implications. Israel found this belief supported by their own experience; how much more should those who know the Lord Jesus Christ, for, as he says, to have seen him is to have seen the Father (John 14:9), is to have witnessed the mercy and compassion of our God.

'My soul, give thanks to the Lord, all my being, bless his holy name. My soul, give thanks to the Lord and never forget all his blessings.'

The natural response to such a Credo is thanksgiving. The psalmist calls upon his 'soul', all that is within him, to 'give thanks', his whole 'being' to 'bless his holy name' and, once more, his 'soul' never to 'forget' the innumerable 'blessings' that have been received.

'It is he who forgives all your guilt, who heals every one of your ills, who redeems your life from the grave, who crowns you with love and compassion.'

Among the most remarkable of those blessings is not only God's unending readiness to forgive, but also the nature of his forgiveness. He does not merely remove the 'guilt' of sin; he 'heals' us of the after-effects of sin; he 'redeems' us from Sheol, or, as we might translate it in this context, from eternal death; and he 'crowns' us with grace, the fruit of his 'love' and compassion.

'His wrath will come to an end; he will not be angry for ever. He does not treat us according to our sins nor repay us according to our faults.'

Though our sins may have earned God's 'wrath' – the psalmist's rather human way of speaking of sin as an offence against God – yet the anger doesn't last long; for the consoling truth is that he does not deal with us as we deserve, does not pay us back in accordance with the scale of our faults. He longs to forgive more than we desire to be forgiven.

'For as the heavens are high above the earth so strong is his love for those who fear him. As far as the east is from the west so far does he remove our sins.'

In an attempt to describe this amazing forgiveness, the psalmist paints the picture of a love which is tall as 'the heavens are high above the earth' and wide as 'the east is from the west': he simply could not cast away our sins further than he does. In the light of this extraordinary forgiving love of God, it is understandable that in today's gospel Jesus should urge us to forgive those who have offended us, thereby showing ourselves to be true children of our Father in heaven.

LET US PRAY: *Lord, when I find myself angry with others, give me a heart filled with your gentle goodness and compassion; give me lips that speak of peace and a mind that reflects your own reconciling love.*

Twenty-Fifth Sunday in Ordinary Time

'My thoughts are not your thoughts, my ways not your ways.' These wise words from the first reading (Isaiah 55:6-9) were meant to encourage exiles to trust in God's plans for them. They also summarise the theme of today's Mass.

The gospel story (Matthew 20:1-16) probably disturbs us: we cannot understand our Lord's approval of a master who pays the latecomer as much as he pays those who have worked hard and long. But then this parable is about the ways of our God; his actions are not according to strict justice, as we see it – if they were, where would any of us be? – but justice softened by compassion and mercy. Why should we be angry if he chooses to be generous?

Doubtless Paul, too, had difficulty in understanding the Lord's ways, but he does not hesitate (Philippians 1:20-24, 27) to seek the Lord's will, whatever it may be. As he puts it, all that matters is that we avoid 'anything… that would be unworthy of the gospel of Christ'.

Psalm 144, from which today's responsorial psalm is drawn, is a song of praise to God for his love and generosity towards us and all his creation, though in fact the scale of his magnanimity is beyond our understanding.

Prayerful Ponderings

'I will bless you day after day and praise your name for ever. The Lord is great, highly to be praised, his greatness cannot be measured.'

The psalmist experiences an urgent need to 'bless' and 'praise' God, not simply from time to time, not only when he is in the mood, but each day, 'day after day' and 'for ever'. God's 'greatness' is simply beyond our understanding or our telling; is it any wonder that we cannot compass his thoughts or comprehend his ways? It has been noted that the Lord's Prayer contains echoes of this psalm. We pray to a Father 'who art in heaven', utterly beyond our human understanding. Our task and our privilege is the hallowing of his 'name'.

'The Lord is kind and full of compassion, slow to anger, abounding in love. How good is the Lord to all, compassionate to all his creatures.'

Once again we meet that Credo of belief in God's gentleness and compassion which served as the refrain for last week's responsorial psalm. Nor are his goodness and compassion reserved for any particular group: they are for 'all his creatures' – even for those whom we may regard as being beyond the pale. Long before Jesus became man and people saw in him 'the reflection of God's glory' (Hebrews 1:3), some glimmer of understanding of the 'divine portrait' had already filtered into the psalmist's mind and filled him with the desire to make praise of God an abiding feature of life.

'The Lord is just in all his ways and loving in all his deeds.'
There are times when we are mystified by the 'ways' of God; we wonder why he allows tragedies to happen, or how he can offer a 'loving' response to all who call upon him, or whether there isn't some limit to his generosity. The answer to these questions is not an apologetic argument but an act of faith: an unshakeable belief – as today's gospel implies – that in fact God 'is just in all his ways' and it is his love that is the ultimate explanation of 'all his deeds'.

'He is close to all who call him, who call on him from their hearts.'
When you have confessed belief in such a heavenly Father, it is not difficult to believe that he is always near, above all to those 'who call on him from their hearts'.

LET US PRAY: *Great God and Father, on those days when we are baffled by your ways, bewildered by your thoughts, may this psalm help us to grow in appreciation of your radiant goodness and compassion and in confidence in the justice of all that you do.*

Twenty-Sixth Sunday in Ordinary Time

Our God, the prophet Ezekiel assures us (18:25-28), does not dwell upon our past, nor does he hold against us the faults of those who went before us. Anyone who repents of sin will be offered the gift of life.

The gospel (Matthew 21:28-32) also speaks of God's readiness to forgive those who recognise the error of their ways and repent; but it is genuine obedience, not lip-service, that he looks for. That's why there is hope for the tax-collector and the prostitute.

Psalm 24 is made up of petitions for God's help and assertions of trust in him. The verses chosen for today's responsorial psalm have a link with the other Scripture readings for they sing of the compassionate love and mercy of God, and pray that he will 'not remember' past sins.

Paul (Philippians 2:1-11) calls upon the warring factions at Philippi to have the mind of Christ who in love for us 'emptied himself… even to accepting death… on a cross'. His self-emptying love is to be the standard for his followers.

Prayerful Ponderings

'Lord, make me know your ways. Lord, teach me your paths. Make me walk in your truth, and teach me: for you are God my saviour.'

The plea to 'know' the Lord's 'ways' and be taught his 'paths' is not simply a request for knowledge or information, the sort of material that could be picked up from a human teacher or gleaned from a book. It is rather a request, on the one hand, for that insight, that God-given way of seeing things, that enables a person, almost instinctively, to recognise what is pleasing to the Lord, and, on the other, for the strengthening grace to pursue it. The psalmist recognises God as 'saviour' and speaks of his 'ways' and of walking in his 'truth'; it might almost be a foreshadowing of the day when Jesus, our saviour God, would declare that he himself is the Way (to whom we are to be committed), the Truth (about God, about humanity, about the world) and the Life (who shares his own life with all who believe in him).

'Remember your mercy, Lord, and the love you have shown from of old.'

'Remember your mercy, Lord' is used as the refrain for today's responsorial psalm. In fact in this and the following verse there is a plea that God will 'remember' two things. The first is altogether positive – his covenant 'mercy' and 'love'. They have characterised his dealings with his people 'from of old'; may they characterise his dealings with his people – and with his psalmist – still.

'Do not remember the sins of my youth. In your love remember me, because of your goodness, O Lord.'
And now for the negative – 'do not remember the sins of my youth'. It is perhaps a prayer that many of us would want to say: conscious of past infidelities, we want them to be forgotten, in the sense that they no longer stand between us and God, that they have been swallowed up by his mercy. And here there is an obvious link with today's gospel. The son who said he would not obey his father, in the end did so, whereas the apparently obedient son proved himself to be completely disobedient. And from that story, Jesus draws the heartening lesson that past failings, however serious, will not be held against us provided that we repent and strive to serve him faithfully. In his compassionate love he does not remember my 'sins', but he does remember 'me'.

'The Lord is good and upright. He shows the path to those who stray, he guides the humble in the right path; he teaches his way to the poor.'
In the light of this psalm's message, we rejoice in a 'Lord' who is 'good' and 'upright', who shows limitless patience in calling back 'those who stray', guiding 'in the right path' those who are truly 'humble', and instructing in 'his way' those who are 'poor' (perhaps especially those who are spiritually poor).

LET US PRAY: *Make us ever mindful of your mercy and compassion, Lord God, so that we may never doubt your readiness to forgive; but make us, at the same time, sons and daughters who seek to be obedient to your will in all things.*

Twenty-Seventh Sunday in Ordinary Time

One of the most frequently used biblical images for God's people is that of the vine/vineyard. The first reading (Isaiah 5:1-7) sadly records that though God lavished so much care upon his people, they failed to respond and so the threat of disaster hangs over them.

The excerpt from Psalm 79, today's responsorial psalm, takes up the same theme. It is an appeal to God that he will 'turn again' towards his vineyard and reinstate it.

A vineyard appears in the gospel (Matthew 21:33-43), too, but this time it is not the vineyard but its tenants who are reproached, because not only do they deprive the owner of his produce but, worse still, they murder his beloved son. The Pharisees are not slow to get the message!

The second reading (Philippians 4:6-9) offers advice which, if followed, will ensure that Christians do not disappoint the Master: they are to pray and be filled with gratitude, they are to pursue all that is true, noble, good, pure, etc.

Prayerful Ponderings

'The vineyard of the Lord is the House of Israel.'
These words, which make up the refrain of the responsorial psalm, do not belong to the psalm itself but are taken from the first reading, and so link up with God's lament over his people, as outlined by Isaiah. But of course we cannot (dare not) forget that Christ's Church, or, more specifically, Christ himself is the vine, and that if we, the branches, fail to live in him, we shall not bear fruit but will wither away (John 15:1-17).

'You brought a vine out of Egypt; to plant it you drove out the nations. It stretched out its branches to the sea, to the Great River it stretched out its shoots.'
The psalmist recalls how God rescued 'a vine', his people, 'from Egypt' and planted it in its own land, after disposing of 'the [pagan] nations' who dwelt there. Since then, it has grown immensely, pushing out its 'branches' till they reach, to the west, the Mediterranean 'sea' and, to the east, the 'Great River' Euphrates. Expressed in Christian categories, this verse speaks of the rescuing work of Christ, the Exodus from sin and hell, that his saving death has won for us, and also of the miraculous spread of the Church so that in the space of a few centuries it had become the religion of the Roman Empire.

'Then why have you broken down its walls? It is plucked by all who pass by. It is ravaged by the boar of the forest, devoured by the beasts of the field.'

In words reminiscent of Isaiah's – though a good deal more daring – the psalmist wants to know how God could have allowed disaster to overtake his vine, so that its protective 'walls' are 'broken down' and it has become a prey for enemies, presented in the guise of devouring 'beasts'. Throughout Christian history there have often been times when the followers of Christ have been shaken by scandals in their midst or by persecution or by a falling away of interest in the Church. It is not too difficult for us to empathise with the psalmist and repeat his 'why?' to the Lord.

'God of hosts, turn again, we implore, look down from heaven and see. Visit this vine and protect it, the vine your right hand has planted.'

After the 'why?' of incredulity comes the ardent plea for help from the 'God of hosts'. Again with some daring, he is called upon to 'turn again', which is tantamount to a request that he should repent: he should 'look down' and see what is happening, should return to his former way of treating his 'vine' and so 'protect' it.

'And we shall never forsake you again: give us life that we may call upon your name.'

Some scholars suggest that the 'turn again' of the previous verse might refer not so much to God as to the psalmist and the psalmist's compatriots; it is they who must repent and so the prayer is equivalent to 'turn us again', give us the grace of conversion. This understanding seems to be borne out by the present verse with its promise that 'we shall never forsake you again' and that, if you restore us to life, we shall 'call upon' you in prayer.

'God of hosts, bring us back; let your face shine on us and we shall be saved.'
Whatever the precise meaning the prophet had in mind, we rightly plead that God in his compassion will 'bring us back' to him, allow his 'face' to 'shine on us' with love and so enable us to be 'saved'.

LET US PRAY: *Lord Jesus, you are the Vine, we are the branches; may we always be firmly rooted in you through faith and prayer and obedience to your word, and when scandals rock your Church, may we see that as a sign that we must turn back to you with renewed fervour and trust.*

Twenty-Eighth Sunday in Ordinary Time

The Jewish people, even in dangerous and difficult times, believed that God would finally triumph; and so the outcome of the final battle between good and evil depicted by Isaiah (25:6-10) is that God is victorious and spreads a luscious banquet for all his people.

Once again Psalm 22 makes its appearance as the day's responsorial psalm, though it is particularly its final verses, with their reference to hospitality, that are relevant to the other Scripture readings.

The gospel (Matthew 22:1-14) speaks of the Messianic feast, prepared by the Shepherd-King; unhappily, some of the guests refuse to come, while others come inappropriately dressed for such an occasion.

Paul (Philippians 4:12-14, 19-20), writing from prison, speaks of his own indifference in the face of poverty or riches, but at the same time thanks his friends at Philippi for their gifts and prays that God will amply reward them.

Prayerful Ponderings

The famous Baptist preacher Charles H. Spurgeon described today's psalm as 'the pearl of the psalms'. Certainly, it is hard to think of any other that has enjoyed greater popularity; though perhaps it is not always realised that it envisages the Lord not only as caring shepherd but also as gracious host. (Strictly speaking, they are probably not two distinct images but rather two aspects of the same image: the shepherding of the Lord includes many other activities beyond those expected of ordinary shepherds. However, in the following comments, I will comment exclusively on the host aspect.)

The fact that today's response, **'In the Lord's own house shall I dwell for ever and ever'**, is taken from the latter part of the psalm, suggests that it is the image of host, rather than that of shepherd, that we are meant to focus our attention upon. That would also provide a link with the first reading and the gospel, both of which speak of a divinely provided banquet.

'You have prepared a banquet for me in the sight of my foes. My head you have anointed with oil; my cup is overflowing.' Generous hospitality was typical of the ancient Israelites, just as it is of many modern Bedouin tribes. Even for a stranger, a table was spread and 'oil' and perfume were used to anoint the head. ('In the sight of my foes' is perhaps a reference to the custom whereby a person received into a Bedouin's tent is now safe from his or her foes, however close they may be. Those who are guests of the Good Shepherd are still more surely protected from their enemies.) Hospitality is advocated in the New Testament, too, (for example, 'do not neglect to show hospitality to strangers' [Hebrews 13:2]) and is numbered among the works of mercy by which ultimately we are to be judged. However, the most generous of human hospitality is but a pale reflection of the hospitality extended to us by our God. In the context of the Mass he prepares for us the eucharistic 'banquet' where we eat the bread of everlasting life, and drink from the 'overflowing cup' of the Precious Blood; and the mention of perfumed 'oil', a symbol of rejoicing and festivity, is a further reminder, if that were needed, that the Mass is a uniquely glorious celebration.

'Surely goodness and kindness shall follow me all the days of my life. In the Lord's own house shall I dwell for ever and ever.'

Every time we gather together to offer the Eucharist, to be the guests of the divine host, we are implicitly given a promise that God's 'goodness and kindness' will attend us always. His 'kindness' (*hesed*) means his abiding faithfulness to his covenant, a covenant which he made in his blood, and his 'goodness' indicates the practical acts of friendship which flow from that covenant. To have been the recipient of his hospitality is already the guarantee of our being with him, at the heavenly banquet (Revelation 19:1-11), 'for ever and ever'.

LET US PRAY: *Lord God, we give you heartfelt thanks for the sacred banquet in which Christ is received as our food, the memory of his passion recalled, the mind filled with grace and a pledge of future glory given us (after St Thomas Aquinas).*

Twenty-Ninth Sunday in Ordinary Time

The excerpt from Isaiah (45:1, 4-6) is doubly fascinating: first because it reveals that God is 'the Lord, unrivalled', whose rule extends not simply to Israel but to all nations; and secondly because the Persian king, Cyrus, who was to defeat the Babylonians and eventually release Israel from exile, is spoken of as an instrument in his hands.

The verses from Psalm 95 call for worship to be given to the 'Lord of all the earth', the King before whom 'the gods of the heathens are naught'.

Jesus (Matthew 22:15-21) cleverly avoids a trap, aimed at exposing him either as a rebel in the eyes of the Romans or a collaborator in the eyes of the Jews. He declares that while the state enjoys legitimate authority ('give back to Caesar what belongs to Caesar'), God's absolute power has also to be respected ('and to God what belongs to God').

The second reading, taken from the earliest writing of the New Testament (1 Thesssalonians 1:1-5), speaks of the power of the good news and of the Holy Spirit which brought the Christians of Thessalonika into union with the Father through Jesus Christ, and filled them with faith, hope and love.

Prayerful Ponderings

'O sing a new song to the Lord, sing to the Lord all the earth.
Tell among the nations his glory and his wonders among all
the peoples.'

This psalm is one of a group of hymns that praise 'the Lord' for his
universal reign. The invitation to sing a song that is 'new' suggests
that we should remain alert: in the coming verses we are to hear a
revelation, in the form of a description of the kingship of the Lord.
Because his kingship is universal in its scope, 'all the earth' and 'all
the peoples' are called as witnesses of his 'glory' and 'wonders'.

'The Lord is great and worthy of praise, to be feared above all
gods; the gods of the heathens are naught. It was the Lord
who made the heavens.'

The psalmist expresses the dignity of the heavenly King in a series
of simple statements: he is 'great'; all that we associate with
greatness can be attributed to him. Thus, he is 'worthy of praise' in
a way that no one else could ever be; he is 'to be feared' in the sense
that he is to be held in deepest reverence because of his
overwhelming greatness. In the psalmist's day, each nation claimed
to have its own 'god'; without entering into a theological dispute
about such a claim, the psalmist simply asserts that all of these so-
called 'gods' rank as 'naught' when set against the Lord. The

ultimate reason why this is so is because the Lord is Creator; he and he alone 'made the heavens'.

'Give the Lord, you families of peoples, give the Lord glory and power, give the Lord the glory of his name. Bring an offering and enter his courts.'
In view of the awesome nature of the Lord and his reign, the whole world, all 'families of peoples', are called upon to acknowledge him, give praise for his 'glory' and 'power' (or, his glorious power), and for his glorious 'name'. His name, in this context, refers particularly to the Lord in his royal splendour. There seems to be a certain urgency in the request; note in this verse, and the next, the threefold 'give' and the series of commands, piled one upon another: 'give', 'bring', 'enter', 'worship', 'tremble' and 'proclaim'.

'Worship the Lord in his temple. O earth, tremble before him. Proclaim to the nations: "God is king." He will judge the peoples in fairness.'
The final sentence of the previous verse surely goes with this one. People are commanded to 'enter his courts', the courts of the Temple, and to 'bring an offering' with them, just as the subjects of an earthly king might come into his presence armed with appropriate gifts. They are to 'worship', in a spirit of trembling before his towering majesty. And then, the climax of the psalm: a cry goes up, 'God is king', the sort of cry that might be heard at the coronation of a king. It is he who will sit in judgement, but always 'in fairness', on all 'the peoples'. In recounting how, after David conquered Jerusalem, the ark of the covenant was brought there in triumph, the book of Chronicles quotes almost the whole of this

psalm; was that because the arrival of the ark was like the enthronement of God in the midst of his people (1 Chronicles 16)? As Christians it is our privilege to welcome the King of kings into our hearts and to worship him there, for we are his temple.

LET US PRAY: *Gladly, Lord, we give to you what belongs to you, as our King and God: our praise, our gratitude, our loyalty, our love; and we pray that we may help to make you known, worshipped and loved by all the world.*

Thirtieth Sunday
in Ordinary Time

The opening reading (Exodus 22:20-26) breathes a compassionate concern for the poor, the defenceless, the lowly, reflecting the compassionate concern of God himself.

Care for the less fortunate members of society was one of the special obligations of the king in Israel. The responsorial psalm, a brief passage from Psalm 17, is one of a group known as the royal songs of thanksgiving. In giving thanks for all that God has done for him, the anointed king thinks perhaps especially of his God-given power to help others.

In the gospel (Matthew 22:34-40), Jesus the anointed one, the Messiah, makes it clear that practical love of neighbour is inextricably linked with love of God. It is a message he teaches not only by word but also by example

Paul (1 Thessalonians 1:5-10) has words of praise for the Christians at Thessalonika because they have become 'imitators of... the Lord', receiving the word, despite all difficulties, with 'the joy of the Holy Spirit'.

Prayerful Ponderings

'I love you, Lord, my strength, my rock, my fortress, my saviour.' With the psalmist, we are invited to give expression to our love of God and to recognise that no single word can convey all that he means to us. He is the source of our 'strength'; without him we can do nothing. He is our 'rock', firm, unchanging, utterly reliable; and, as Jesus reminded us, the wise person is careful to build not on sand but on solid rock (Matthew 7:24-27). He is our 'fortress', the one in whom we find refuge, in whom we are kept safe. He is our 'saviour', the Messiah who through death and resurrection has made us his brothers and sisters, heirs to heaven.

'My God is the rock where I take refuge; my shield, my mighty help, my stronghold.'
The search for a suitable way of describing 'my God' – the very word 'my' speaks of intimacy – continues. Again, he is 'the rock where I take refuge'; in her joy at the birth of Samuel, his mother Hannah cried out: 'There is no Rock like our God' (1 Samuel 2:2). Throughout the Hebrew Scriptures God is frequently spoken of as the solid protective 'rock', which keeps us safe. And of course in the New Testament Jesus gives his disciple the name 'Peter', because that disciple is the rock on which he will build his Church and no power will overcome it (see Matthew 16:16-19). The attempt to picture God continues: he is our 'shield', like the huge protective shield which covers a person from head to foot. To sum up, he is our 'mighty help' and our 'stronghold'.

'The Lord is worthy of all praise: when I call I am saved from my foes.'

After the rush of metaphors for God with which this psalm begins and which is without parallel elsewhere in the Psalter, it hardly needs to be said that such a God 'is worthy of all praise' and that 'when I call' upon him, I am confident that I shall be 'saved from my foes', whoever or whatever they may be.

'Long life to the Lord, my rock! Praised be the God who saves me. He has given great victories to his king and shown his love for his anointed.'

These lines appear towards the end of this psalm, one of the longest in the Psalter. In it is described an epic struggle in which the 'king' has been involved but which has ended in triumph for him, because God has 'shown his love for his anointed', and now the king wishes to express his gratitude. A version of the psalm is given in 2 Samuel 22 and there it is attributed to King David. However, in Christian tradition the King, the anointed One, of Psalm 17, is none other than Jesus, the Lord. And so we give thanks for his victory and for our share in it. But as we do so, we must not forget that loving the Lord cannot be divorced from love of our neighbours, especially those who most need our help.

LET US PRAY: *Words can never describe all that you mean to us, dear Lord and God; but we thank you for your wondrous love which expresses itself in so many ways and we beg that we may always be on the lookout for new ways of expressing our love for you, especially in our dealings with 'the least of the sisters and brothers'.*

Thirty-First Sunday
in Ordinary Time

The fifth-century prophet Malachi (Malachi 1:14-2:2, 8-10) does not mince his words: the people, and especially the priests, are reproached for their spiritual negligence; they may go through the motions of religious practice, but they do so without any joy or enthusiasm.

Religious leaders are criticised in the gospel (Matthew 23:1-12) too; Jesus castigates them for being more concerned about drawing attention to themselves than about the message they are to preach.

In striking contrast the second reading (1 Thessalonians 2:7-9, 13) presents Paul as a truly devoted pastor, enthusiastic, hard-working, full of love for his people.

To follow Christ is to serve him humbly; and humility, together with complete trust in God, is the theme of Psalm 130, today's responsorial psalm. It's a psalm which, according to one of the great commentators on the psalms, 'deserves to be classed with the most beautiful psalms of the Psalter'.

Prayerful Ponderings

'Keep my soul in peace before you, O Lord.'
These words are the refrain for this most gentle of psalms, filled perhaps more than any other with the spirit of the gospel, the spirit of humility and childlike trust in God. Like Thérèse of Lisieux, the author of this psalm (a woman, perhaps, who had the experience of holding a weaned child in her arms [see below]) might have said: 'What pleases God in my soul is my littleness and poverty.'

'O Lord, my heart is not proud nor haughty my eyes. I have not gone after things too great nor marvels beyond me.'
First, the negative aspect of accepting one's insignificance: the psalmist has not allowed her 'heart' to be 'proud' or her 'eyes' to be raised in 'haughty' fashion; put simply, she has not pursued 'great things' or 'marvels' beyond her status. In the Psalter, 'great' and marvellous deeds usually refer to God's own saving activities; so this is the psalmist's way of denying that she ever attempts to play God.

'Truly I have set my soul in silence and peace. A weaned child on its mother's breast, even so is my soul.'
Now, in striking contrast, the positive aspect of things: a 'soul' which has quietened itself (literally, abased itself) so that it can rest unruffled in God 'in silence and peace'. It's a situation movingly compared to that of a 'weaned child on its mother's breast', a child

which no longer seeks nourishment from its mother but simply finds its joy in lying close to her heart. Like the psalmist, we are invited to entrust ourselves in peaceful surrender to our God. In the measure that we do so, we shall avoid the empty religious practices which are rebuked in today's first reading and in the gospel.

'O Israel, hope in the Lord both now and for ever.'
All that has gone before has been the prayer of an individual, but now that individual calls upon all who will hear, that they too may have the personal experience of placing all their 'hope in the Lord', of being with the Lord like a child with its mother in good times and bad 'now and for ever'. We cannot allow this psalm to speak to us without recalling our Lord's own warning that there can be no place for us in the kingdom unless we become as little children (Matthew 18:1-5). Again, it's helpful to reflect on the sentiments that must have filled Mary's heart as she sang this little psalm while cradling the Christ-child in her arms!

LET US PRAY: *Lord God, you are both Father and Mother to us; we beg you to help us to be sincere and joyful in the practice of our faith, and to experience in prayer the joy of being like a child in its mother's arms.*

Thirty-Second Sunday in Ordinary Time

As the year is drawing to its close, so life itself will one day come to an end. Today's first reading, taken from the last book of the Old Testament to be written (Wisdom 6:12-16), urges us to seek true wisdom, which is presented as a woman of many attractive qualities, and, later in the book, as a manifestation of God himself.

Appropriately, the responsorial psalm, taken from Psalm 62, speaks of the soul's longing for God who is Wisdom itself.

The first Christians were deeply concerned about the coming of Christ at the end of time and the implications of that coming. Paul discusses these issues frequently in his letters to the Thessalonians, as in the passage that forms today's second reading (1 Thessalonians 4:13-18).

The gospel (Matthew 25:1-13) insists that, since the hour of his coming is uncertain, wise people, like wise bridesmaids, 'stay awake', so that they will be ready for the arrival of the Bridegroom.

Prayerful Ponderings

'O God, you are my God, for you I long; for you my soul is thirsting. My body pines for you like a dry, weary land without water.'

From earliest times this psalm has been used in the Morning Prayer of the Church. What a wonderful way to begin a new day! Here is a psalm which speaks eloquently of the depth of our desire for God. He is 'my' God – there is a personal relationship between us. My yearning for him is expressed in a series of simple but vivid expressions: I 'long' for him, 'my soul is thirsting' for him, 'my body pines' for him; every fibre of my being needs him. As long as that yearning is unsatisfied, I can best compare myself to a piece of 'land without water' – 'dry, weary', empty.

'So I gaze on you in the sanctuary to see your strength and your glory. For your love is better than life, my lips will speak your praise.'

The psalmist seeks refuge from an empty world, where God seems far away, by coming to the 'sanctuary', in the hope of recapturing the vision of God's 'strength and glory'. Of course we don't have to go to the sanctuary of a church in order to discover God. It is enough that we seek him in the sanctuary of our own hearts; there we recognise once more that 'your love' (not my love for him but his for me) is the most valuable thing in life. What could be wiser, then, than that 'my lips' should constantly 'speak [his] praise'?

'So I will bless you all my life, in your name I will lift up my hands. My soul shall be filled as with a banquet, my mouth shall praise you with joy.'

The conclusion of the previous verse is reinforced by this one: since God matters so much to me, then it is my resolve to 'bless [him] all my life', to 'lift up my hands' to him in prayer. I know that in this way my empty soul 'shall be filled as with a banquet'. Of course prayer is seldom all sweetness, but even when it is difficult and demanding it will still be my 'joy' to 'praise you'.

'On my bed I remember you. On you I muse through the night for you have been my help; in the shadow of your wings I rejoice.'

Prayer in the evening, as well as in the morning, is what might be expected of those who take God seriously, for it is not only during daylight hours but also during the hours of darkness – even 'on my bed' – that they wish to remain close to him. Unlike the psalmist, we may not be able to 'muse' and meditate on him 'through the night' – it is important that we get our sleep! – but nonetheless we are confident that we are always under 'the shadow of [his] wings' (like a chick protected by a mother bird) and that is cause for rejoicing.

LET US PRAY: *Lord our God, give us the wisdom to long for you with all our hearts and to seek you constantly in prayer, and so, when this life draws to a close, may we be ready for that face-to-face meeting with you which will satisfy all the deepest longings and yearnings of our hearts.*

Thirty-Third Sunday in Ordinary Time

Again, thoughts of Christ's final coming and the wisdom to be ready for it are the concerns of this Sunday's readings. We all have received various gifts and abilities, symbolised in the gospel (Matthew 25:14-30) by the silver coins known as 'talents'. They are God's gifts that have been entrusted to us and only if we use them wisely for his glory can we look forward to hearing his welcoming words on the Last Day.

According to the first reading (Proverbs 31:10-13, 19-20, 30-31), wisdom is to be found above all in the home; there the good wife shows her wisdom by making good use of her talents and abilities for the benefit of the whole family. It is in the ordinary events of human living that we win blessings with the Lord.

Psalm 127, today's responsorial psalm, speaks of the blessings received by the person 'who fears the Lord', and, by implication, uses wisely his or her God-given gifts. Since it focuses particularly on the blessings of family life, it has obvious links with the first reading.

Paul tells us in the second reading not to be worrying about the wrong questions – such as, 'When will the Last Day come?' (1 Thessalonians 5:1-6) – but rather to be intent upon living as people who are making ready for that coming, whenever it may be.

Prayerful Ponderings

'O blessed are those who fear the Lord and walk in his ways! By the labour of your hands you shall eat. You will be happy and prosper.'
The 'blessed' or truly 'happy' people are those who have the spirit of reverence and obedience towards the Lord, 'those who fear the Lord and walk in his ways'. In Old Testament times one of the surest ways in which a man showed reverence and obedience was by being a good father and husband, and so by working hard for the sake of his family and ensuring that their basic needs were met. The change in wording, from 'those' (plural) to 'you' (singular), seems to be the poet's way of saying that he is directing his words to each individual who reads or listens to his poem. Of course, not every person who uses this poem will be married; and even for those who are, the relationships between husband and wife are very different nowadays from what they once were: it may be the woman, for example, who goes out to work and the man who stays at home as the 'house-husband'. However, the underlying message is for everyone: it is in the daily living out of the vocation to which we have been called that we can best show that we 'fear' the Lord and reverence 'his ways'.

'Your wife like a fruitful vine in the heart of your house; your children like shoots of the olive, around your table.'
The thoughts of the previous verse are further elaborated. Though domestic relationships may have changed in all sorts of ways – not

all of them for the best – it is still true that few blessings can compare with that of happy family life. There the wife, the 'fruitful vine', sees her children gathered around the 'table' like so many 'olive' plants, tender growths to be cared for and nurtured, to be taught in their turn to reverence and obey the Lord. They are the hope of the future.

'Indeed thus shall be blessed the man who fears the Lord. May the Lord bless you from Zion in a happy Jerusalem all the days of your life.'
This psalm is one of a group that seems to have been sung by pilgrims as they made their way up to 'Zion' (another word for 'Jerusalem') for the celebration of the great feasts. It was the ideal occasion for instruction. They are taught that the wise person who 'fears the Lord', and proves it by the way he or she lives daily life, is assured of a blessing. At this point the psalm widens its scope to address the whole people: may they all experience the blessings of the Lord 'from Zion'. We too are a pilgrimage people and, during these final days of the year when our thoughts turn towards the end of the journey, this little psalm teaches us that the wisdom which best prepares us for the coming of Christ is that which leads us, whatever our way of life, to offer faithful service to the Lord and to our sisters and brothers.

LET US PRAY: *Lord our God, bless us your pilgrim people as we make our journey through life; may we so reverence your name and follow your ways, that we may be brought to our heavenly home where, in the company of Mary our Mother and all your family of saints, we may enjoy perfect happiness for ever.*

Solemnity of Christ the King

Today we arrive at the grand finale of the Church's liturgical year, the feast of Christ the King, and all the readings reflect that fact, not least the responsorial psalm, Psalm 22, with its unforgettable picture of the Shepherd-King.

The first reading (Ezekiel 34:11-12, 15-17) tells how the leaders, the shepherds of Israel, have failed their people and so, the Lord promises, he himself will come and shepherd them. While he will care for his people in every way, he will also be ready to 'judge' them when appropriate.

It is the judging aspect of Christ the King that is underlined in the gospel, which sets before us the famous judgement scene of Matthew (25:31-46). Jesus comes at the end of time as Universal King who is also Judge; like a shepherd, he will separate sheep from goats, depending upon whether people have expressed loving care for others, especially 'the least of these brothers [and sisters] of mine', or have failed to do so.

After the final judgement, Paul teaches (1 Corinthians 15:20-26, 28), when everything will have been subjected to Christ, then Christ himself will surrender 'the kingdom' to his Father 'so that God may be all in all'.

Prayerful Ponderings

For the fourth time this year – see 4th Sunday of Lent, 4th Sunday of Easter and 28th Sunday in Ordinary Time – it is Psalm 22 that provides our responsorial psalm, with the refrain 'The Lord is my shepherd; there is nothing I shall want.' (Verse four, which speaks of 'the valley of darkness', is omitted, though it is difficult to understand why, particularly in view of its reference to 'crook' and 'staff' [see below].) On this occasion the choice of Psalm 22 has surely been determined by the fact that in ancient Israel, and in the Near East generally, the word 'shepherd' was used not only in its obvious pastoral sense but also in a political sense: it was applied to leaders, such as kings, royal officials, elders, anyone who had authority. It was even applied to gods.

However, almost every time that 'shepherd' is used of Israel's leaders, it is used in a critical sense (see today's first reading): they lead the sheep astray, neglect them, are unfaithful, seek their own interests. In striking contrast, the Lord is presented as their true Shepherd: in the Psalter he is described as leading them 'like a flock', bringing forth 'his people like sheep' and guiding 'them through the desert' (Psalm 77:52); and carrying them like a shepherd (Psalm 27:9).

But of course the classic description of the Lord as Shepherd-King of Israel is to be found in Psalm 22. There he is depicted as:

- **meeting** all my real needs (not necessarily in the way I think he ought!);
- **providing** me with food and drink;
- **guiding** me along the right path; being always with me, even 'in the valley of darkness', his shepherd's crook and his royal 'staff' (sceptre) in his hand;
- **preparing** a glorious 'banquet' for me, where he treats me as an honoured guest;
- **assuring** me that his 'goodness and kindness' will be with me always until I reach 'the Lord's own house' where 'I shall dwell for ever and ever'.

Wonderful though this description is, there is something more wonderful still – our Lord's incredible words: 'I am the good shepherd' (John 10:11); they tell us that in the person of Jesus Christ we actually catch sight of the Good Shepherd, the one who fulfils all that was expected of a worthy shepherd and more besides: who freely laid down his life for us, his sheep.

What a glorious Shepherd-King we worship this day!

LET US PRAY: *Father, as we celebrate today's great feast, we renew our pledge of lifelong fidelity to our Shepherd-King; may we so serve him in the persons of our sisters and brothers that we may belong to his eternal kingdom of 'truth and life, of holiness and grace, of justice, love and peace'.*

OTHER FEASTS
that may be celebrated on a Sunday

Praise
O servants
of the
Lord

The Ascension of the Lord

This festival has been celebrated with full solemnity since the fourth century as the final, glorious manifestation of our Lord's Easter exaltation, and Sunday by Sunday we profess our belief that 'he ascended into heaven'.

On this day, in each year of the three-year cycle, the first reading is always the same; it is the story of the ascension, as recounted by Luke in the Acts of the Apostles (1:1-11). Having instructed the apostles over a period of forty days, Jesus promises them the gift of the Holy Spirit, assures them that they are to be his witnesses 'to the ends of the earth' and then is lifted up until hidden from their sight by a cloud. As they gaze into the sky, an angel reminds them that until the day when Jesus returns, they have a job to do.

The nature of that job is specified in the gospel (Matthew 28:16-20). Jesus, who by his paschal victory has mounted his throne in heaven and shown himself to be 'great king of all the earth', now commissions his disciples (and us in our turn) to take the good news of the gospel and the rebirth of baptism to the peoples of all nations. The Church of its very nature will forever be a missionary Church.

The passage from St Paul (Ephesians 1:17-23), which gives us our second reading today, is a prayer that we may be enlightened to appreciate the glorious hope that is ours. God has exercised his infinite power by raising Jesus from the dead and seating him at his right hand in heaven. That same power is exercised on our behalf so that we may enter into the glorious kingdom.

Psalm 46, from which today's responsorial psalm is drawn, was originally used as part of a solemn procession, perhaps one that brought the ark of the covenant, the sign of God's presence, into the Temple. There may even have been some kind of enthronement ceremony in recognition of God's everlasting kingship.

Prayerful Ponderings

'All peoples, clap your hands, cry to God with shouts of joy! For the Lord, the Most High, we must fear, great king over all the earth.'

If in days gone by the people of Israel were encouraged to 'clap [their] hands' and 'cry ... with shouts of joy' as they saw the ark of the covenant being borne in solemn procession to the Temple, how much more should we be encouraged to celebrate on this great day – even if our celebrations are a little more subdued – when we honour our Lord's being lifted up from this earth and borne into heaven itself. The Scripture readings we've heard today make it clear that everything possible must be done to ensure that one day 'all peoples' will join in our Ascension Day celebrations: with us they will honour a king who, though like to us in all things, is in fact 'the Lord, the Most High', a king whom 'we must fear', not because he is a tyrant but because he is so awesome and great. Such a one is by right 'great king over all the earth'.

'God goes up with shouts of joy; the Lord goes up with trumpet blast.'

It's hard to listen to these words, which make up the refrain of today's responsorial psalm, without sensing that something special is happening: they take us to the heart of the celebration. There's 'joy' in the air; besides the rhythmic clapping (see previous verse) and the shouts of delight, there is the sound of the 'trumpet', the ram's-horn trumpet (*shophar*) whose 'blast' marks important occasions, such as the New Year (Numbers 29:1) or the accession of a king (2 Kings 9:13) or, most significantly in this context, the occasion when David brought the ark to the city to make Jerusalem into God's abode (2 Samuel 6:15). And when the people proclaimed in this psalm: 'God goes up', 'the Lord goes up', was it part of a dramatised renewal (perhaps an annual renewal) of the first time the ark entered the Temple? And did they actually see the ark once more mounting towards the doors of the Temple where it would be enthroned? In any event today, through the liturgy, the ascension of the Lord is truly re-presented in our midst so that, with the eyes of faith, we see our Lord returning to the Father's house, and with joy we can cry out that the Lord does indeed go up.

'Sing praise for God, sing praise, sing praise to our king, sing praise. God is king of all the earth. Sing praise with all your skill.'

Again and again, again and again, the cry goes up: 'Sing praise'. We have all heard a crowd giving vent to its feelings, not necessarily bad ones, by repeating some brief catchphrase over and over again. The very insistence of the cry to praise God in this psalm – 'sing praise for' him, 'sing praise to' him – suggests that it served a similar purpose, and it's easy to visualise the whole assembly chanting these words which sum up the sentiments of all. On this day a similar cry goes out from the Church: we are all invited to raise our voices in praise of the Lord, who has been raised to his heavenly throne as 'king of all the earth'.

'God is king over the nations; God reigns on his holy throne.' Though praise of God is important, even vital, yet by itself it is not enough. We cannot, dare not, forget that Jesus' final word to his disciples on the day of his ascension was in the form of their commissioning: their task was to be his witnesses, to take his message to the ends of the earth. On each subsequent Ascension Day the Church – and we are the Church – is called upon to renew its efforts to make known that 'God is king over the nations', whether they know it or not, that God reigns over all the earth, and wants his reign to be acknowledged. More even than that, he wants all people to hear the good news that he 'has passed beyond our sight, not to abandon us but to be our hope' (Preface of the Mass for the Ascension).

LET US PRAY: *Lord our God, fill us with joy as we celebrate the ascension into heaven of our Lord Jesus Christ. Help us so to live our lives in this world that others will be brought to know and love him as King and God, and finally, where he, the Head, has already gone, may we, his members, most surely follow. This prayer we make in the name of that same Jesus Christ our Lord.*

The Body and Blood of Christ

In his encyclical 'The Eucharist in its Relationship to the Church', Pope John Paul II wrote 'The Eucharist, as Christ's saving presence in the community of the faithful and its spiritual food, is the most precious possession of the Church' (§9). Each year the Solemnity of the Body and Blood of Christ celebrates this 'most precious possession'. In Year A the focus is particularly on the divine bread, but also on the creative word of God.

In the first reading (Deuteronomy 8:2-3, 14-16), Moses urges the people to remember the Lord's goodness to them in the days of trial as they trudged though the desert on their way to the Promised Land. They came to appreciate the importance of 'everything that comes from the mouth of the Lord'; and they saw how God tended to all their needs; in particular, he 'fed [them] with manna'. In the light of today's feast, we recognise that that manna was but a foretaste of what was to come.

A similar connection is to be found in the responsorial psalm. Psalm 147 is a hymn of praise for all that God has done for his people, in particular for feeding them 'with finest wheat'. On this day we can hardly hear those words without thinking of the Eucharist, the more so when we listen to the gospel (John 6:51-58). There, Jesus reminds his hearers that their ancestors who ate the manna are now dead, but anyone who eats the bread that he offers 'will live for ever'; and 'the bread' that he will give is 'my flesh, for the life of the world'.

Paul, in the second reading (1 Corinthians 10:16-17), teaches his friends at Corinth that sharing the bread of the Eucharist brings us into 'communion with the body of Christ' and at the same time into communion with one another, so that together 'we form a single body'.

Prayerful Ponderings

'O praise the Lord, Jerusalem! Zion, praise your God!'
These words, of which the first part serves as the response to the responsorial psalm, indicate clearly that we are being invited to raise our voices in 'praise' of our 'God'. 'Jerusalem' is personified, addressed as though it were a person, because it stands for all the people of the city; but today it stands for all of us. Of course, human beings do not praise the Lord in order to meet his needs but rather to meet their own. It is they, as creatures, who have the need to praise, to express gratitude, to voice joy at the wonders he has done for them. If praise was called for in Jerusalem of old, how much more in the 'new' Jerusalem, the Church.

'He has strengthened the bars of your gates, he has blessed the children within you. He established peace on your borders, he feeds you with finest wheat.'
We praise and give thanks for all that God has done for his Church. It is he who 'has strengthened' the Church throughout the ages; it is he who, through the sacraments, 'has blessed the [Church's] children'; it is he who despite every storm and tempest has time and again 'established peace' for his people; and it is he, especially, who 'feeds [us] with finest wheat' in the Holy Eucharist.

'He sends out his word to the earth and swiftly runs his command. He makes his word known to Jacob, to Israel his laws and decrees. He has not dealt thus with other nations; he has not taught them his decrees.'

In these few lines there are two references to 'his word' (a third reference occurs in a verse that does not appear in today's responsorial psalm); it 'swiftly runs' to do his bidding. Not only is it a creative word, accomplishing what it is sent to do, but also a revealing word, bringing guidance and instruction to his people.

On this feast day we remember that the Mass is the Liturgy of the Eucharist but also the Liturgy of the Word; that the Lord is as truly present in his Word as in the Sacrament; that the purpose of the Liturgy of the Word is to deepen our faith so that we may benefit to the full from the Liturgy of the Eucharist. Truly, 'he has not dealt thus with other [people]'. Let us give thanks.

LET US PRAY: *In the wonderful sacrament of the Holy Eucharist, Lord Jesus, you speak to us through your word and feed us on the 'finest wheat' of your own Body and Blood. May we, your followers, always be grateful for this most precious possession and through our reception of your Body and Blood may we share ever more fully in your holiness.*

The Presentation
of the Lord (February 2)

Though for many centuries this feast was called the feast of the Purification of the Blessed Virgin Mary, its earlier title, one it had from its origin in the fourth century, was the Presentation of the Lord. The restoration of that title is a reminder that, like all Marian feasts, this one points to the indestructible link between Mary and her Son: it is through her that he is presented.

When Mary presents the Child, the prophecy of Malachi (3:1-4) is fulfilled, for he speaks of a day when 'the Lord will enter his Temple' – though he could never have believed that the Lord would arrive in the form of a babe-in-arms!

The second reading, taken from the letter to the Hebrews (2:14-18), underlines the reality of our Lord's humanity. Like any other first-born Jewish child, he had to be 'redeemed' forty days after his birth; like any one of us, he had to grow to maturity and, like any one of us, he was tried and tempted.

The gospel story (Luke 2:22-40) is something more than a bare account of the way in which Mary and Joseph complied with the Law. It serves as a formal announcement of Jesus' arrival in the Temple, his presentation to his people and, still more, his presentation to Jews and Gentiles alike as 'the salvation' of all humankind.

The second half of Psalm 23 is this Sunday's responsorial psalm. The earlier part speaks of the Lord as Maker and King of all creation and provides instruction on those who may worthily enter his presence; this part is applied to the arrival of the Lord himself in the Temple.

Prayerful Ponderings

'O gates, lift up your heads; grow higher, ancient doors. Let him enter, the king of glory!'

It seems likely that this psalm, especially this part of it, was composed as an accompaniment for a procession in which the ark of the covenant, the symbol of the Lord's presence, would be solemnly brought to the Temple, and there a festival celebrated in honour of his Kingship. In poetic language, the huge 'gates' which stand at the threshold of the Temple are commanded to 'lift up [their] heads' and the 'ancient doors' to 'grow higher', as though the entrance needs to be enlarged if it is to cope with the towering figure of the invisible Lord who is about to enter his palace, seated upon the ark as upon a throne. Nothing must be allowed to hinder the entry of 'the king of glory'.

'Who is the king of glory? The Lord, the mighty, the valiant, the Lord, the valiant in war.'

We can perhaps imagine the priests calling out, from inside the Temple, 'Who is [this] king of glory?', and back coming the response: 'The Lord, the mighty, the valiant'. We may find it difficult to feel sympathy for such a warlike God! However, the fact is that especially in earlier times the God of Israel was regarded as a mighty warrior: after all, he was more powerful than the pagan gods, and they, according to their adherents, had brought creation into being after the defeat of fierce enemies, and so, it was sometimes argued, Yahweh must have done the same; again, the people of Israel were confident that he had accompanied them, riding on the ark (which served as his chariot), when they went out to battle, so that they confidently styled him 'valiant in war'. Under the influence of the prophets these warlike titles came to take on a more general significance: they were ways of pointing to his greatness, his power, his holiness.

'O gates, lift high your heads; grow higher, ancient doors. Let him enter, the king of glory!'

Once more the cry is raised that the gateway be enlarged to allow entry to 'the king of glory'. This time we might listen to it against the backcloth of today's feast. In the arms of Mary and Joseph, Jesus is coming to his Temple, coming to present himself as our Redeemer, 'the salvation ... for all the nations', the one who restores us to God's friendship, the one who stands not only as 'the glory of ... Israel' but also as 'a light ... to the Gentiles' (hence, today's candle ceremony). And we are being invited to open the doors of our hearts to him, to rid ourselves of whatever might stand in the way of his coming, to enable him to become for us 'the king of glory'.

'Who is he, the king of glory? He, the Lord of armies, he is the king of glory.'

If the repeated query about the identity of 'the king of glory' again results in a warlike response, 'the Lord of armies', we have only to look at the tiny child in the arms of Mary and Joseph to realise that many faulty views about God stand in need of revision as a result of the incarnation. Ever since this child was born in the stable at Bethlehem, forty days ago, we have been gently reminded that our God is 'the king of glory' not only because he is all-powerful but also because he is so humble as to 'empty himself' and become 'completely like his brothers [and sisters]' (second reading). It is precisely through this self-emptying even to death on a cross that he has conquered in the only battle that matters, that against sin and Satan, and so set us free. Significantly, though the response to today's psalm is based on this verse, and its earlier counterpart, the answer it gives to 'Who is the king of glory?' makes no mention of military prowess; it states quite simply: 'It is the Lord.'

LET US PRAY: *Jesus, Son of God and Son of Mary, you are Lord. Come into our hearts, defeat all our spiritual enemies and be now and for ever our King of glory.*

Birth of John the Baptist

(June 24)

Four passages in Isaiah speak of a mysterious 'servant' of the Lord who suffers much but is the bearer of God's good news. Christian tradition has applied them to Jesus, but today's liturgy applies the second of them to John the Baptist, called as God's servant 'from my mother's womb', commissioned to bring Israel back to God and destined to be 'the light of the nations' (Isaiah 49:1-6).

The second reading (Acts 13:22-26), from Paul's sermon to the Jews at Antioch, speaks of John as the one who 'heralded' the coming of the Saviour and 'proclaimed … repentance' which is the precondition of conversion to the Lord.

The subjects of today's gospel (Luke 1:57-66, 80) are John's birth, the wonder surrounding his naming and the 'awe' which filled those present, leading them to wonder: 'What will this child turn out to be?'

Psalm 138, 'The Hound of Heaven' psalm, as it has been called, is a most appropriate psalm for today's feast, with its reference to God's knowledge and power which affect even those as yet unborn.

Prayerful Ponderings

'O Lord, you search me and you know me, you know my resting and my rising, you discern my purpose from afar. You mark when I walk or lie down, all my ways lie open to you.' This awesome and attractive psalm – unfortunately, only a few of its verses appear in the responsorial psalm – acclaims the unique character of God's knowledge, power and presence. John the Baptist, whose birth we celebrate today, must often have reflected on the wonderful relationship that existed between himself and God. Perhaps in the last dark days of his life, when he was being held captive in a subterranean dungeon by King Herod, he would have prayed this psalm, confident that God's discerning eye, which had always been upon him, was upon him still; that God's knowledge extended to even the most mundane of his everyday activities, such as 'my resting' and 'my rising', 'when I walk' and 'when I lie down'; that God's ability to read the human heart enabled him to 'discern my purpose from afar' – it was clear to God even before it was properly formed in the herald's own mind. However, this psalm is not just for great saints or for those who play an obviously crucial role in the Lord's plans; it is for everyone. Each of us can give thanks that our God is so close, that his loving knowledge of us is so all-embracing, that his understanding of us and our plans is so complete, that 'all [our] ways lie open' before him.

'For it was you who created my being, knit me together in my mother's womb.'

The words of the psalmist would have been particularly apt on the lips of John the Baptist, for he was born in answer to his parents' fervent prayers, even though both were old and Elizabeth 'was barren'. Not only John's birth and the events surrounding his circumcision, but even the fact of his conception, must have caused the people to marvel and to wonder aloud: 'What will this child [so obviously due to God's intervention] turn out to be?' However, again we are invited to recognise that 'it was [the Lord] who created my being', it was he who 'knit me together in my mother's womb'. I am unique: not an accident but part of God's great design.

'I thank you for the wonder of my being, for the wonders of all your creation.'

Even the psalmist could appreciate the incredible craftsmanship that goes into the fashioning of a human being. And so the psalmist felt the need to thank God 'for the wonder of my being'; and that act of gratitude led on to a prayer of thanks for 'the wonders of all your creation'. Today we know so much more about the wonder of a human being – scientists have even mapped the human genome ('the language in which God created life', as President Clinton described it) – and yet perhaps there is still nothing so calculated to fill us with wonder as the sight of a new-born baby. People tend to express their astonishment as they take hold, for example, of the child's tiny fingers, and say with a sense of awe: 'Isn't he perfect! Isn't she wonderful!' Each of us is one of 'the wonders of [his] creation'; but through Jesus, whose coming was heralded by John, a still greater wonder has been worked in us: we have been re-created as sons and daughters of God.

'Already you knew my soul, my body held no secret from you when I was being fashioned in secret and moulded in the depths of the earth.'

This verse summarises what has gone before: it tells how we are known through and through, 'soul' and 'body', by the God who made us. Even when we were being 'moulded in the depths of the earth', a metaphor for the hiddenness of the womb, we 'held no secret from [him]'. It is indeed a cause for wonder and gratitude that he who made the stars and the seas and the earth, was also involved in our prenatal development, fashioning us down to the tiniest detail so that we are, as the RSV translation puts it, 'intricately woven'. Again we need to remind ourselves on this day that God's creative work is involved in the fashioning not only of the great saints like John the Baptist but also of every single human being who is ever conceived.

LET US PRAY: *God our Father, on this day as we rejoice in the birth of John the Baptist, herald of our Saviour, we give thanks that through the saving work of Jesus Christ we, who are wondrously made, have become sharers in his divine Sonship.*

Saints Peter and Paul
(June 29)

Today's first reading (Acts 12:1-11) records how, when Peter was imprisoned, 'the Church prayed to God for him unremittingly' and how he was miraculously released.

Paul is able to make the proud boast: 'I have fought the good fight to the end... I have kept the faith.' But he acknowledges that it was the Lord who 'rescued [him] from the lion's mouth' and prays that glory may be given to him for ever (2 Timothy 4:6-8, 17-18).

The gospel (Matthew 16:13-19) is the account of Peter's recognition of Jesus as 'the Christ' and Jesus' designation of Peter as the rock on which 'I will build my Church'.

Today's psalm is taken from the first part of a song of thanksgiving (Psalm 33) which praises God, in particular for the psalmist's own experience of deliverance.

Prayerful Ponderings

'I will bless the Lord at all times, his praise always on my lips; in the Lord my soul shall make its boast. The humble shall hear and be glad.'

The psalmist boldly proclaims his resolve to 'bless the Lord at all times', to have 'his praise always on my lips', to ensure that only 'in the Lord my soul shall make its boast'. Moreover, it is his belief that 'the humble', those who are attuned to the Lord's ways, will rejoice with him and 'be glad' when they 'hear' what the Lord has done for him. Such sentiments would surely be dear to the heart of St Paul for he was a truly grateful man. In the first of his letters which has come down to us, he urges his friends in Thessalonika to give thanks to the Lord 'in all circumstances' (1 Thessalonians 5:18). The implication is that that is what he did himself; indeed, the notion of thanksgiving occurs so many times in his subsequent correspondence that it might well be described as one of his theme songs.

'Glorify the Lord with me. Together let us praise his name. I sought the Lord and he answered me; from all my terrors he set me free.'

Both Peter and Paul could look back on situations where they had been set free 'from all [their] terrors' by the intervention of the Lord. Peter was 'sprung' from his prison cell (first reading) despite the elaborate precautions taken against his escape, and Paul recalls how he was 'rescued from the lion's mouth' (though we have no means of knowing what – or who – the 'lion' may have been). So each might have urged the other to 'glorify the Lord with me. Together let us praise his name.' However, on this feast day we are all being invited to join them in glorifying, praising and thanking the Lord for all that he has done through these two great apostles. Once they had discovered, or, better, been discovered by, Christ and recognised him as Lord, they sought him and his will all the rest of their days. Many times they had to face 'terrors' – in the end they had to face the threat of death itself for his sake and that of the gospel – and still they remained confident that 'he [would] set [them] free'.

'Look towards him and be radiant; let your faces not be abashed. This poor man called; the Lord heard him and rescued him from all his distress.'
No one can 'look towards [the Lord]' with faith and trust without becoming 'radiant', without catching a certain likeness to him; it is what Paul seems to be referring to when he says that 'all of us, with unveiled face, seeing the glory of the Lord … are being transformed into the same image from one degree of glory to another' (2 Corinthians 3:18). The apostles would have us know that despite our weakness we need not 'be abashed'; like many a 'poor man [who has] called [on the Lord]', we can be sure that the Lord will hear and will rescue us from 'all [our] distress'.

'The angel of the Lord is encamped around those who revere him, to rescue them. Taste and see that the Lord is good. He is happy who seeks refuge in him.'

Often in the Hebrew Scriptures the expression 'the angel of the Lord' is used of God himself, particularly when he intervenes in human affairs. His presence is like a protective army 'encamped around those who revere him'; he is ready 'to rescue them', whatever their plight. The psalmist's advice is straightforward: 'Taste and see that the Lord is good'; it is as though he were saying: I've given my testimony, now it's up to you to sample the Lord for yourself; then you'll discover that you are safe in his hands. That discovery was certainly made by the two saints we honour today: they are foundations on which the Church rests. Finally, it's worth noting that the advice to 'taste and see that the Lord is good' is applied in the New Testament to Christians who have newly received the sacrament of baptism (1 Peter 2:3), while among the early Fathers of the Church it is also used in reference to the Holy Eucharist.

LET US PRAY: *We pray, Lord our God, that the Church throughout the world may be inspired by the noble apostles Peter and Paul and that, like them, all Christians may taste and experience your unbounded goodness and all-powerful protection.*

The Transfiguration
of the Lord (August 6)

Written when the Jews were reeling under Syrian persecution, the first reading, from the book of Daniel (7:9-10, 13-14), offers encouragement by reminding them, on the one hand, of God in the guise of 'one of great age' ablaze with glory, and, on the other, of God's representative, 'one like a son of man' on whom 'sovereignty, glory and kingship' are conferred and who is worshipped by all the nations. It is that representative who is at the centre of today's feast.

Peter, to whom the second reading (2 Peter 1:16-19) is attributed, recalls that what Christians believe are not 'cleverly invented myths' but events of which he, and others, were witnesses. And so, he claims, 'we were with him on the holy mountain' (of transfiguration).

The gospel for this feast (Matthew 17:1-9) is always an account of the transfiguration, but, depending upon which year it is within the three-yearly cycle, the passage is taken either from the Gospel of Matthew or that of Mark or that of Luke.

Psalm 96 is one of the 'enthronement psalms', praising God for his universal reign, but also emphasising the fact that he has saved his people.

Prayerful Ponderings

'The Lord is king, let earth rejoice, let all the coastlands be glad. Cloud and darkness are his raiment; his throne, justice and right.'

Much of the imagery in this psalm seems to have been borrowed from the religions of surrounding nations which commonly depicted their 'god' achieving kingship by defeating lesser 'gods' in battle. The psalm begins with a simple but powerful statement – 'the Lord is king' – which will be elaborated in the rest of the song, though in fact only a few verses appear in today's responsorial psalm. To begin with, his kingship is an invitation to the whole 'earth' to 'rejoice' and 'all the coastlands' to 'be glad'. Mysterious 'cloud and darkness' both conceal him and serve as signs of his presence, just as they had been on Mount Sinai (and of course on the mount of transfiguration when Jesus was overshadowed by a bright cloud [see gospel]); they are even looked upon as 'his raiment', his royal robes, while the 'throne' on which he is seated has as its bases 'justice and right'. A royal throne has always been a symbol of kingship, and the Lord's throne could not be more firmly based, for it rests on the twin qualities of justice and right. Justice embraces all those divine actions and decisions which lead to righteousness, to a way of life that is rich and fulfilling.

'The mountains melt like wax before the Lord of all the earth. The skies proclaim his justice; all peoples see his glory.'

Next, the very 'mountains', despite their apparently immovable solidity, are compared to a piece of 'wax' melting away in the overwhelming presence of 'the [mighty] Lord of all the earth'. Meanwhile 'the skies' take up the proclamation of 'his justice': he is a judge who can be depended upon always to act with fairness and impartiality. And finally there is the promise that 'all peoples' will 'see his glory'. On the mount of transfiguration the apostles saw their Master so utterly open to the Father that the Father's glory shone through his person and his very garments, while the voice of the Father proclaimed him as his beloved Son. In the liturgy of today's feast we too are granted a vision of our Lord in glory, one truly like us – 'one like a son of man' as Daniel describes him (first reading) – but at the same time one on whom has been conferred 'sovereignty, glory and kingship'.

'For you indeed are the Lord, most high above all the earth, exalted far above all spirits.'

The refrain of today's psalm is made up of a phrase from this verse of the psalm – 'most high above all the earth' – prefaced by the exclamation 'the Lord is king'. To hail Jesus as Lord is already to hail him as king, is already to acknowledge that he is 'exalted far above' not only all earth and all people but also 'above all spirits'. On this day we are filled with wonder for we see how the Jesus who walked the streets of Palestine has been revealed as glorious image of the Father and as supreme Lord of all creation. He stands for us 'as a lamp for lighting a way through the dark until the dawn [of our resurrection] comes and the morning star rises' (second reading).

LET US PRAY: *We bow down in wonder before you, Lord Jesus, truly the only Son of the Father but also our brother, like to us in all things but sin. As you have shared our common lot of suffering and even of death, so may we one day share in full measure in your heavenly glory.*

The Assumption of the Blessed Virgin Mary (August 15)

The first reading (Revelation 11:19; 12:1-6,10) comes from a type of literature (apocalyptic) which aimed to give reassurance in time of persecution. 'The woman' it speaks of refers in the first place to the Church: she will survive the Roman offensive that has been mounted against her. But it is also applied to Mary who is mother of the Messiah, mother of the Church and first and most perfect Christian disciple.

Through Christ, the second Adam, has come the hope of resurrection from the dead; he is the first to rise in glory; today's feast teaches us that Mary was the second to share his triumph to the full and is a pledge for us of the resurrection that awaits us beyond death (1 Corinthians 15:20-26).

The gospel for today (Luke 1:39-56) tells the delightful story of the Visitation; it is a story which revolves around the woman who is to bring us our Messiah. Through him will come salvation and the promise of resurrection from the dead. Today we rejoice in the belief that the promise has already been fulfilled – in the Assumption of Mary, body and soul, into the glory of heaven.

Psalm 44, which provides the two verses which make up today's responsorial psalm, was originally a wedding song for a Davidic king but later came to be recognised as Messianic, as achieving its fulfilment in the Davidic king, Jesus Christ; the 'queen' who is shown standing beside him is applied in today's feast to Mary taken up into the heavenly palace of her Son.

Prayerful Ponderings

'The daughters of kings are among your loved ones. On your right stands the queen in gold of Ophir.'

A royal wedding was always an important event and this psalm reflects the magnificence of such an occasion. Extravagant praise is lavished on the king: 'your ladies of honour' (the translation which the RSV prefers to 'your loved ones') are members of royal families, they are in fact 'the daughters of kings'. But 'on [his] right' in the place of honour – and this is the climax of the passage – 'stands the queen' herself. She is dressed in beautiful robes interwoven with glistening 'gold of Ophir', the most costly gold that could be found. All eyes are on the bride: 'on your right stands the queen, in garments of gold' is the refrain of today's psalm. We too are meant to fix our eyes upon her, seeing in her the completed model, so to say, of what we all shall be one day, provided only that we are faithful to the Lord. The reference to her vesture of gold might remind us of the many blessings with which God has clothed her to prepare her to be a worthy mother of his Son. However, it is because she responded so wholeheartedly with those graces that she is the symbol of the Church. Moreover, she knows how indebted she is: for ever she will acknowledge (see the Magnificat in today's gospel) 'the Almighty has done great things for me. Holy is his name.'

'Listen, O daughter, give ear to my words: forget your own people and your father's house.'

The king begs his new queen ('daughter', he calls her) to 'give ear to my words', in the double sense of listening carefully to them and acting upon them; in the gospel Mary is portrayed precisely as someone who 'pondered' in her heart all that happened to her, all that was said to her, and at the same time was always ready to respond as the humble handmaid of the Lord. According to this verse, the queen is also called upon to 'forget [her] own people and [her] father's house'. In its original context this rather extreme advice perhaps meant little more than that she must give up her own home and family and enter the king's abode, become part of his family and be totally devoted to him. (It has been suggested that she was a foreign princess and so would literally have had to leave her home and family behind.) Mary, too, in becoming mother of the Saviour, had to set out on a new way of life: everything must have been so different for her, perhaps she had to abandon her plans to marry Joseph, certainly she had to be prepared to follow her Son wherever it might take her – even to the summit of Calvary.

'So will the king desire your beauty: he is your lord, pay homage to him.'

'The king' of the psalm may well have been overwhelmed by the physical 'beauty' of his young wife, but it was above all the spiritual beauty of Mary that was so pleasing to the Lord. The queen of the psalm was also reminded that her husband was her 'lord' and that therefore she must 'pay homage to him' – in the days of the psalmist a wife's submission to her husband was taken for granted – but Mary had no need to be reminded of her duties to the Lord; her whole life was shot through with praise, she desired only to 'magnify the Lord' in all that she did. As the first and perfect Christian she gladly paid him homage.

'They are escorted amid gladness and joy; they pass within the palace of the king.'
The mysterious 'they' of this verse are the queen's bridesmaids. They have known her perhaps from childhood and it is a moment of immense 'gladness and joy' when the solemn moment arrives for the bridal pair and their attendants solemnly to enter 'the palace of the king'. A new life has begun. On this day we celebrate Mary's solemn entry into the palace of the King of kings; but she does not go alone. She is the first of all those who will share her triumph – who, like her, will be taken up body and soul into the glory of heaven.

LET US PRAY: *We beg you, Mary our Mother, to pray for us that, following your example, we may serve the Lord faithfully all our days and at the last enjoy eternal gladness and joy in the palace of Jesus, our Lord and King.*

The Triumph
of the Cross (September 14)

Today's first reading (Numbers 21:4-9) takes us back to Israel's days in the desert. There, because of their rebellion against God, 'fiery serpents' were let loose upon them. Many died. Moses was instructed to erect a bronze serpent on a pole; whoever looked upon it would live.

The gospel (John 3:13-17) draws a striking parallel between the raising up of the serpent in the desert and the lifting up of Jesus on the cross 'so that everyone who believes in him may... have eternal life'.

The second reading (Philippians 2:6-11) is the beautiful hymn from St Paul's letter to the Philippians which records how Jesus, putting aside his glory, humbled himself to the point of death – even death on a cross. By his obedience our rebellions are healed.

The verses which make up today's responsorial psalm are taken from the lengthy Psalm 77 (no less than 70-odd verses long!), one of three great historical psalms which tell the story of God's dealing with his people, especially at the Exodus, during their desert journeyings and on their arrival in the Promised Land.

Prayerful Ponderings

'Never forget the deeds of the Lord.'
A nation forgetful of its own past has been likened to a person suffering from loss of memory. The people of Israel were never in danger of such amnesia because biblical faith is a 'remembering' faith, a faith rooted in history (Guttiérez), a faith which will 'never' allow the people to 'forget the deeds of the Lord'. Though these words are not an exact excerpt from today's psalm, they do in fact serve as a perfect summary of it, for time and again throughout the song the importance of remembering is underlined.

'Give heed, my people, to my teaching; turn your ear to the words of my mouth. I will open my mouth in a parable and reveal hidden lessons of the past.'
The opening words of the psalm itself are usually described as 'wisdom instruction'. The 'wise men' or sages in the ancient Near East were renowned for their discernment and teaching ability. They would expect the 'people' to 'give heed... to my teaching', would call upon them to 'turn [their] ear to the words of my mouth' and would promise to speak to them 'in a parable' (or wise saying) and in particular to 'reveal [to them] hidden lessons of the past'. On this day we are invited to be wise enough to listen carefully to the history of our ancestors in faith, for we too have much to learn from it.

'When he slew them then they would seek him, return and seek him in earnest. They would remember that God was their rock, God the Most High their redeemer.'

After the introductory verse, we are led at once to a later section of the psalm which is concerned with the desert wanderings of the people of Israel. Despite all that God had done in rescuing them from slavery in Egypt, they had chosen to murmur against him (first reading), to rebel against him. Then, when he took action against them ('he slew them' is the way the psalmist describes it), 'they would seek him' again, they would 'return and seek him in earnest'. They 'would remember' – the very thing that we are all asked to do today – remember that he is 'their rock', their abiding support, that he is 'God the Most High', that he is 'their redeemer'.

'But the words they spoke were mere flattery; they lied to him with their lips. For their hearts were not truly with him; they were not faithful to his covenant.'

However, their display of repentance, apparently so earnest, was completely deceptive, for 'the words they spoke were mere flattery'. The situation is not unlike that addressed by the prophet Hosea when he told the people, in God's name: 'Your love is like a morning cloud, like the dew that goes away early' (6:4). All that they had said 'with their lips' were so many lies because there was no real repentance, 'their hearts were not truly with him' and that was shown by the way they lived their lives: quite simply, 'they were not faithful to his covenant'. However, on this feast day especially, we dare not forget that we too, despite all our promises and good intentions, continue to fail the Lord in so many ways. As St James reminds us, we still have to learn how to be 'doers of the word and not merely hearers who deceive themselves' (James 1:22).

'Yet he who is full of compassion forgave their sin and spared them. So often he held back his anger when he might have stirred up his rage.'

Thankfully, our God does not treat us as we deserve, for he 'is full of compassion'; just as he 'forgave their sin' and 'spared' his people, so he continues to spare us and forgive us. The psalmist remarks – it sounds almost in unbelief – that 'so often he held back his anger' when what might have been expected was that he would 'have stirred up his rage'. Still more do we have reason to marvel at the long-suffering compassion of our God; over and over again we have to confess our failures and sins – that's the way we begin almost every Mass – and yet we have confidence to believe that he will have mercy and spare us. That lonely figure, hoisted up on the cross of Calvary, is the reason for our hope. If he is prepared to lower himself to this level (see second reading) in order to save us, then we can indeed look up to him in faith and be confident that we shall be healed, no matter how terrible our unfaithfulness.

LET US PRAY: *Lord, may we heed the wise words of the psalmist; may we never forget your mighty deeds and never lose heart in your compassion and your readiness to save; may we recognise the cross of Calvary as the symbol not of tragedy but of glorious triumph.*

All Saints
(November 1)

The first reading (Revelation 7:2-4, 9-14) speaks of the countless host of men and women from every time and place who now see the face of God.

John (1 John 3:1-3) gives us the incredible news that already we are 'God's children' but that we are destined to 'be [still more] like him because we shall see him as he really is'.

In the Beatitudes (Matthew 5:1-12), Jesus speaks of the happiness, the blessedness, of those who are poor, who are gentle, etc. By earthly standards such people may seem to be losers but in fact they are the children of God, destined for 'the kingdom of heaven'.

Psalm 23 is a hymn in honour of the Kingship of the Lord; the verses used for the responsorial psalm are, appropriately for today's feast, in the form of an entrance liturgy, announcing the kind of people who will be allowed into the presence of God.

Prayerful Ponderings

'The Lord's is the earth and its fullness, the world and all its peoples. It is he who set it on the seas; on the waters he made it firm.'

This opening verse sets the scene for all that follows; we are introduced to the Lord, to whom belongs the whole of nature, 'the earth and its fullness', and the whole of humanity, 'the world and all its peoples'. All belongs to him because he is the great creator. In the psalmist's day the world was pictured as being surrounded on all sides by a watery waste, and God himself as conquering the fierce waters, so that he is able to 'set [the world] on the seas', to fix it on stout pillars so that it will remain 'firm' and secure amidst 'the [heaving, chaotic] waters' of the deep. This is the God whom the pilgrims are now about to approach.

'Who shall climb the mountain of the Lord? Who shall stand in his holy place?'

In the light of the poet's description of the mighty creative work of God, an obvious question arises: Who would ever be worthy to 'stand in his holy place', to enter into the presence of a God such as this? Of course the psalmist is thinking only in terms of the Temple in Jerusalem: before pilgrims ascend 'the mountain' on which the Temple is built, they wonder who will be able to 'climb the mountain of the Lord' with good conscience. However, on this feast day, the question is a more extraordinary one: Who dare think of entry into God's temple in heaven, entry into the very presence of God himself?

'The man with clean hands and pure heart, who desires not worthless things. He shall receive blessings from the Lord and reward from the God who saves him.'

The psalmist tries to answer the first question raised by the previous verse, as to who might worthily make his or her way into the Temple. But the answer, provided in all probability by one of the temple personnel, may also be accommodated to the second question, which is concerned with those worthy of entrance into heaven itself. It is those who have 'clean hands and pure heart' because they do no wrong to others and above all because they have set their hearts on the Lord rather than on any 'worthless things'. They are the people spoken of in the first reading: those who have been faithful to God through every trial, who 'have washed their robes white ... in the blood of the Lamb'. They are the beatitude people spoken of in the gospel: those who have known their need of God, those who are gentle, those who hunger and thirst for what is right, those who are merciful, those who are peacemakers, those single-minded people who are described by Jesus as 'the pure of heart' and the children of God. Even on earth they bore the likeness of the Lord because of the way they lived their lives and today we celebrate the fact that they are still more wonderfully 'like him' because now they 'see him as he really is' (second reading). The promise has indeed been fulfilled: they have received 'blessings from the Lord' and a 'reward' beyond their wildest dreams. But they will always remember that their eternal reward is due not to themselves but rather to 'the God who saves them'.

'Such are the men who seek him, seek the face of the God of Jacob.'

This verse is also the refrain for today's responsorial psalm. In its original setting it was simply a confirmation that those approaching the Temple were worthy to enter. But today we might use it in the form of a prayer: we are the people 'who seek [you]', we are the people who 'seek [your] face'. The psalm may suggest that those worthy of God's presence are completely perfect, and maybe the readings seem to confirm that same impression. However, among the saints whom we honour today are people whom we have known and loved; many of them are 'ordinary' people, with their weaknesses and defects and sinfulness. They have striven hard but ultimately they are in heaven because of the mercy of God. And the same will be true of ourselves. Despite all our inadequacies – and worse – our hearts are set on God; we do long to see his face and we do trust that he will one day enable us to join that countless throng gathered before his throne.

LET US PRAY: *Great and mighty God, we praise you on this day for all the wonders of your creation but still more for the wonders of spiritual re-creation which you have worked in your saints. We too seek your face; may there come a time when we shall be numbered among those who are honoured on the feast of All Saints.*

The Dedication of the Lateran Basilica (November 9)

Today's feast commemorates the dedication of the Mother Church of Christendom: St John Lateran is the Pope's own cathedral church. The first reading (Ezekiel 47:1-2, 8-9, 12), with its account of a stream of water flowing from the Temple and bringing life wherever it flows, is meant to remind us of the blessings that God bestows upon people everywhere through his Church.

Paul (1 Corinthians 3:9-11, 16-17) describes the Church as a living temple; it is a sacred temple, indwelt by the Holy Spirit and with Jesus Christ as its sole foundation.

In response to those who attack him for his cleansing of the Temple in Jerusalem, Jesus speaks of himself as a sanctuary which, three days after its destruction, he will raise up (John 2:13-22).

Psalm 45 is the first of a group of psalms which hymn the glory of Jerusalem, the Lord's own city. It is because his Temple is founded there that it will stand firm against every assault. Verses from this 'song of Zion' feature in today's Mass: Jesus dwells for ever in his Church.

Prayerful Ponderings

'God is for us a refuge and strength, a helper close at hand, in time of distress: so we shall not fear though the earth should rock, though the mountains fall into the depths of the sea.'

A psalm could hardly begin with a more powerful confession of trust in God. He is saluted as 'a refuge and strength', one who defends us and empowers us in our difficulties, and as one always ready to help us for he is 'a helper close at hand, in time of distress'. In response to such statements of confidence, 'we', the people gathered in worship, declare that 'we shall not fear', not even if those apparently most stable elements, the earth and the mountains, should come to grief. We shall not fear 'though the earth [itself] should rock' and the burly mountains totter and 'fall into the depths of the sea'. St John Lateran is the Pope's own church, and, as an inscription at its east end explains, it is 'Mother and Head of All Churches… throughout the world'. And so on this feast day we are meant to give thanks for the world-wide unity of the Church, a unity which centres around the Holy Father. It was after proclaiming Peter as 'the rock on which I will build my church' that Jesus promised that, despite enemies from without and scandals from within, his Church would stand firm for ever, and that not even 'the gates of hell' would prevail against it (Matthew 16:18).

'The waters of a river give joy to God's city, the holy place where the Most High dwells. God is within, it cannot be shaken; God will help it at the dawning of the day.'

The mysterious reference to 'the waters of a river' perhaps reflects an ancient belief that the home of the gods is surrounded by a stream which serves as a life-giving source. There is a similar allusion in the description of the river flowing out of the garden of Eden in Genesis 2:10-12, as well as in the account of the life-giving stream in today's first reading. Jerusalem is 'God's city' and 'the holy place where the Most High dwells'; it is his presence that ensures its security against all its enemies; 'at the dawning of the day', when enemies often decide to mount an attack, he will be there to help and protect it. On this feast day we remember with gratitude that the survival of the Church throughout the ages – 'it cannot be shaken' to destruction – is ultimately due to the fact that it stands in the world as the city of God; it is he who dwells in its midst, it is he who ensures that while it is always in need of reform it is also a source of health and holiness for the whole human race.

'The Lord of hosts is with us: the God of Jacob is our stronghold. Come, consider the works of the Lord, the redoubtable deeds he has done on the earth.'

The cry 'the Lord of hosts is with us' is a confident declaration that God with his heavenly army of angels is there to defend us. It is not anything we can do that gives us our security, but the fact that he 'is our stronghold'. We have only to consider 'the works of the Lord', says the psalmist, only to reflect on 'the redoubtable deeds he has done on the earth' and, it seems to be implied, we shall have no reason to fear. No doubt the psalmist is thinking of all that God has done for his people throughout their history, beginning with the Exodus from Egypt. But today when we profess our trust in the God who dwells within his Church, we recall 'the redoubtable deeds' that Jesus has accomplished from his birth in the stable of Bethlehem, to his public ministry, to his death and glorious resurrection, to his sending of the Holy Spirit so that the Church might spring to life as his Mystical Body. We know that he will be with us 'always, even to the end of the age' (Matthew 28:20).

LET US PRAY: *Lord God, on this day, we give thanks that the Risen Lord is the new Temple in which you are worshipped in spirit and in truth, that we have been built up as living stones in that Temple and that bound together in unity under Peter's successor we can be confident that the Lord of hosts will be with us throughout the ages.*

The Immaculate Conception of the Blessed Virgin Mary (December 8)

From the first reading of this Mass (Genesis 3:9-15, 20) it becomes clear that today's feast links Mary intimately with her Son; it is her role in salvation history that is stressed. The promise, following upon the 'fall' of our first parents, that there would be a woman whose child is destined to crush the head of the 'serpent' already hints at the work accomplished by the Mother and her Child, Mary and Jesus.

The redemptive work of Christ is beautifully outlined in the second reading (Ephesians 1:3-6, 11-12); the richest beneficiary of that work is Mary, whom the Father 'chose in Christ' from all eternity that she might be 'holy and spotless' and so a worthy mother for his Son.

The gospel account of the Annunciation (Luke 1:26-38) shows Mary being greeted by the angel as 'full of grace', a fullness which she has known from the first instant of her existence.

Psalm 97 is an Enthronement Psalm, praising the Lord as King. The verses chosen for today's great feast rejoice in the saving work of God and, by implication, in the part that Mary played in that work as mother of the Saviour.

Prayerful Ponderings

'Sing a new song to the Lord for he has worked wonders. His right hand and his holy arm have brought salvation.'
The first sentence, which is the beginning of Psalm 97 and also the refrain of today's responsorial psalm, is a call to 'sing a new song to the Lord'. The song is new not because it is newly composed but because it is an invitation to consider anew the saving work of the Lord, and on this day especially it is a call to praise God for the unique place he has allotted in his plans to the young maiden, Mary of Nazareth. It is a call addressed to all the redeemed, who have benefited so magnificently from the 'wonders' that 'he has worked' through Jesus (see second reading), wonders which are greater even than those worked at the Exodus. Like a warrior, whose hands and arms overcome the foe, Jesus is pictured as overcoming our deadliest foes, sin and death, by 'his right hand and his holy arm'. However, we cannot forget that his hands were nailed to a wooden beam, his arms stretched on a cross in order to achieve our 'salvation'.

'The Lord has made known his salvation; has shown his justice to the nations. He has remembered his truth and love for the house of Israel.'
The first, as well as the supreme, beneficiary of the Lord's saving work is Mary. In her we see what 'salvation' means: it is not simply

forgiveness of sin or even preservation from sin (as the title of Immaculate Conception might suggest) but rather something gloriously joyful and positive. Mary is 'highly favoured'; from the first moment of her existence she is so intimately united with God that there is no room for sin in her life, so completely his that she is the embodiment of all we mean by 'salvation' (see the gospel). And so, in her, God 'has shown his justice [his plan to draw all men and women into his friendship] to [all] the nations'; in her he has shown forth his steadfast 'love' for his people, 'the house of Israel': he has been true to all his promises of old.

'All the ends of the earth have seen the salvation of our God.'
The story of the garden of Eden tells of human rebellion against God; abusing the wonderful gift of freedom, human creatures make wrong choices and so separate themselves from God and from one another (see first reading). And yet from the beginning God had already planned to come to our rescue so that we could become 'his adopted sons [and daughters]'. Through Jesus, whose very name means 'salvation', the divine plan is revealed to 'the ends of the earth', and, at the heart of that plan, God has shown his immense respect for human freedom: the coming of the Saviour was made dependent upon the free consent of Mary (see the gospel).

'Shout to the Lord all the earth, ring out your joy.'
The responsorial psalm ends in much the same way as it began, with a summons to praise the Lord, though this time we are invited to 'shout to the Lord' and to 'ring out [our] joy', and the summons goes out to 'all the earth'. Today is indeed a celebration, a celebration of God's merciful goodness, his matchless love for his

creatures, but also a celebration of a woman, one of us, who in view of the motherhood that was to be hers was conceived immaculate (God's favour was always with her) and who when the time came was ready to give her wholehearted consent. And so it was that the Word was made flesh and dwelt among us. Alleluia!

LET US PRAY: *Heavenly Father, you chose Mary from all women to be our advocate with you and our pattern of holiness. Following her example, may we always be ready to say a wholehearted Yes to your designs so that, like Mary, we may bring Christ to others and so continue your saving work in the world.*

APPENDIX

Psalms	Sundays/Feasts
1:1-4, 6	6th Ordinary (C)
4:2, 4, 7, 9	3rd Easter (B)
8:4-9	Most Holy Trinity (C)
14:1-5	22nd Ordinary (B)
	16th Ordinary (C)
15:1-2, 5, 7-11	3rd Easter (A)
	13th Ordinary (C)
15:1, 5, 8-11	33rd Ordinary (B)
16:1, 5-6, 8, 15	32nd Ordinary (C)
17:2-4, 47, 51	30th Ordinary (A)
	31st Ordinary (B)
18:8-11	3rd Lent (B)
18:8-10, 12-14	26th Ordinary (B)
18:8-10, 15	3rd Ordinary (C)
21:8-9, 17-20, 23-24	Passion Sunday (A,B,C)
21:26-28, 30-32	5th Easter (B)
22	4th Lent (A)
	4th Easter (A)
	28th Ordinary (A)
	16th Ordinary (B)
22:1-3, 5-6	Christ the King (A)
23:1-6	4th Advent (A)
	All Saints
23:7-10	Presentation of the Lord
24:4-5, 8-9, 10, 14	1st Advent (C)
24:4-9	26th Ordinary (A)
	1st Lent (B)
	3rd Ordinary (B)
26:1, 4, 7-8	7th Easter (A)
26:1, 4, 13-14	3rd Ordinary (A)
26:1, 7-9, 13-14	2nd Lent (C)
28:1-4, 9-10	Baptism of the Lord (A)
29:2, 4-6, 11-13	13th Ordinary (B)
	3rd Easter (C)
	10th Ordinary (C)
30:2-4, 17, 25	9th Ordinary (A)

31:1-2, 5, 7, 11	6th Ordinary (B)
	11th Ordinary (C)
32:1-2, 4-5, 18-19	5th Easter (A)
32:1, 12, 18-20	19th Ordinary (C)
32:2-3, 7, 17-19	30th Ordinary (C)
32:4-5, 18-20, 22	2nd Lent (A)
	29th Ordinary (B)
32:4-6, 9, 18-20, 22	Most Holy Trinity (B)
33:2-7, 9	4th Lent (C)
33:2-9	19th Ordinary (B)
	SS Peter and Paul, Apostles
33:2-3, 10-15, 9	20th Ordinary (B)
33:2-3, 16-23	21st Ordinary (B)
39:2, 4, 7-10	2nd Ordinary (A,B)
39:2-4, 14, 18	20th Ordinary (C)
40:2-5, 13-14	7th Ordinary (B)
44:10-12, 16	Assumption
45:2-3, 5-6, 8-9	Dedication of Lateran Basilica
46:2-3, 6-9	Ascension of the Lord (A,B,C)
49:1-8, 12-15	10th Ordinary (A)
50:3-4, 12-15	5th Lent (B)
50:3-4, 12-13, 17, 19 + Luke 15:18	24th Ordinary (C)
50:3-6, 12-14, 17	1st Lent (A)
53:3-6, 8	25th Ordinary (B)
61:2-3, 6-9	8th Ordinary (A)
62:2-8	32nd Ordinary (A)
62:2-6, 8-9	22nd Ordinary (A)
	12th Ordinary (C)
64:10-14	15th Ordinary (A)
65:1-7, 16, 20	6th Easter (A)
	14th Ordinary (C)
66:2-3, 5, 6, 8	Mary, Mother of God (A,B,C)
	20th Ordinary (A)
66:2-3, 4-8	6th Easter (C)
67:4-7, 10-11	22nd Ordinary (C)
68:8-10, 14, 17, 33-35	12th Ordinary (A)
68:14, 17, 30-31, 33-34, 36-37	15th Ordinary (C)
70:1-6, 15, 17	4th Ordinary (C)

71:1-2, 7-8, 12-13, 17	2nd Advent (A)
71:1-2, 7-8, 10-13	Epiphany (A, B, C)
71:1-2, 7, 34-38	Triumph of the Cross
77:3-4, 23-25, 54	18th Ordinary (B)
79:2-3, 15-16, 18-19	1st Advent (B)
	4th Advent (C)
79:9, 12-16, 19-20	27th Ordinary (A)
80:2-8, 10-11	9th Ordinary (B)
83:2-3, 5-6, 9-10	Holy Family (C)
84:9-12	2nd Advent (B)
84:9-14	19th Ordinary (A)
	15th Ordinary (B)
85:5-6, 9-10, 15-16	16th Ordinary (A)
88:2-3, 16-19	13th Ordinary (A)
88:2-5, 27, 29	4th Advent (B)
89:1, 3-6, 12-14	18th Ordinary (C)
	23rd Ordinary (C)
89:12-17	28th Ordinary (B)
90:1-2, 10-15	1st Lent (C)
91:2-3, 13-16	11th Ordinary (B)
	8th Ordinary (C)
92:1-2, 5	Christ the King (B)
94:1-2, 6-9	3rd Lent (A)
	23rd Ordinary (A)
	4th Ordinary (B)
95:1-3, 11-13	Christmas Midnight (A,B,C)
95:1, 3-5, 7-10	29th Ordinary (A)
	2nd Ordinary (C)
95:1-7	Dedication of the Lateran Basilica
96:1-2, 6-7, 9	7th Easter (C)
96:1-2, 5-6, 9	Transfiguration of the Lord
96:1-2, 6-9	27th Ordinary (C)
96:1, 6, 11-12	Christmas Dawn (A,B,C)
97:1-6	Christmas Day (A,B,C)
97:1-4	6th Easter (B)
	28th Ordinary (C)
	The Immaculate Conception
97:5-9	33rd Ordinary (C)

99:1-3, 5	11th Ordinary (A)
	4th Easter (C)
102:1-2, 11-12, 19-20	7th Easter (B)
102:1-4, 6-8, 11	3rd Lent (C)
102:1-4, 8, 10, 12-13	7th Ordinary (A)
	8th Ordinary (B)
	7th Ordinary (C)
102:1-4, 9-12	24th Ordinary (A)
103:1-4, 24-25, 27-30	Baptism of the Lord (C)
103:1, 24, 29-31, 34	Pentecost (A,B,C)
104:1-6, 8-9	Holy Family (B)
106:23-26, 28-31	12th Ordinary (B)
109:1-4	Body and Blood of Christ (C)
111:4-9	5th Ordinary (A)
112:1-2, 4-8	25th Ordinary (C)
114:1-6, 8-9	24th Ordinary (B)
115:10, 15-19	2nd Lent (B)
115:12-13, 15-18	Body and Blood of Christ (B)
116:1-2 + Mark 16:15	9th Ordinary (C)
	21st Ordinary (C)
117:1-2, 16-17, 22-23	Easter Sunday (A,B,C)
117:2-4, 13-15, 22-24	2nd Easter (A)
117:2-4, 15-18, 22-24	2nd Easter (B)
117:2-4, 22-27	2nd Easter (C)
117:1, 8-9, 21-23, 26, 28-29	4th Easter (B)
118:1-2, 4-5, 17-18, 33-34	6th Ordinary (A)
118:57, 72, 76, 77, 127-130	17th Ordinary (A)
120	28th Ordinary (C)
121:1-2, 4-9	1st Advent (A)
121:1-5	Christ the King (C)
122	14th Ordinary (B)
125	30th Ordinary (B)
	2nd Advent (C)
	5th Lent (C)
127:1-5	Holy Family (A)
	33rd Ordinary (A)
	27th Ordinary (B)
129	5th Lent (A)

	10th Ordinary (B)
130	31st Ordinary (A)
136:1-6	4th Lent (B)
137:1-5, 7-8	5th Ordinary (C)
137:1-3, 6, 8	21st Ordinary (A)
137:1-3, 6-8	17th Ordinary (C)
138:1-3, 13-15	Birth of John the Baptist
144:1-2, 8-11, 13-14	14th Ordinary (A)
	31st Ordinary (C)
144:2-3, 8-9, 17-18	25th Ordinary (A)
144:8-9, 15-18	18th Ordinary (A)
144:8-13	5th Easter (C)
144:10-11, 15-18	17th Ordinary (B)
145:1, 7-10	23rd Ordinary (B)
145:2, 6-10	26th Ordinary (C)
145:2, 7-10	32nd Ordinary (B)
145:6-10	3rd Advent (A)
145:7-10	4th Ordinary (A)
146:1-6	5th Ordinary (B)
147:12-15, 19-20	2nd after Christmas (A,B,C)
	Body and Blood of Christ (A)

Canticles

Isaiah 12:2-6	Baptism of the Lord (B)
	3rd Advent (C)
Daniel 3:32, 52-56	Most Holy Trinity (A)
Luke 1:46-50, 53-54	3rd Advent (B)